Living in La La Land: My Story

by
Diane White

MAPLE
PUBLISHERS

Living in La La Land: My Story

Author: Diane White

Copyright © Diane White (2023)

The right of Diane White to be identified as author of this work has been asserted by the author in accordance with section 77 and 78 of the Copyright, Designs and Patents Act 1988.

First Published in 2023

ISBN 978-1-915996-78-7 (Hardback)
978-1-83538-026-0 (Paperback)
978-1-83538-027-7 (E-Book)

Book layout by:
White Magic Studios
www.whitemagicstudios.co.uk

Published by:
Maple Publishers
Fairbourne Drive, Atterbury,
Milton Keynes,
MK10 9RG, UK
www.maplepublishers.com

Foreword

I think most people believe in fate. I know I do. After working my way around Europe, I had decided to take up an offer from some Aussie girls I'd met in Crete. They had invited me to spend the summer with them in Australia. Fate intervened and I finished up in Los Angeles.

I had every intention of just spending a summer there. That summer turned into a decade. This was the 90's, I know some of you reading this weren't even born yet! You can spend a summer in London, New York or Paris, but be warned Los Angeles is like a magnet, with Beverley Hills being the epicentre of that magnet. It's hard to explain how easy it is to get caught up in the lifestyle, but hopefully after reading my story you will understand why it's called La La Land.

Try to imagine your life being played out on a movie set, every moment seeming surreal. If you can do that you are half way to understanding what living life there is like. Now you are thinking how can a true story about living in Los Angeles for a decade be interesting. Well fifty per cent of my story is about living with the Hilton family in Bel Air. My life living with two precocious girls. A story of parental neglect and emotional turmoil. A vacation from hell and an insight into the rich and famous.

The Hiltons bought a gift store on the Sunset Plaza, a very prestigious area in Beverley Hills. My story is about some of the funny things that happened to me while dealing with the many celebrities that shopped there. Let me name drop a little. Musicians, Bruce Springsteen, Barry Manilow, Maria Carey and Ringo Starr. Actors, Jack Lemmon, Andy Garcia, Sylvester Stallone, Joan Collins, Priscilla Presley and Stephanie Powers to name a few. I have a story to tell about each and every one of them. There is nowhere on earth that someone could have this experience, except in La Land. So, this place stole ten years of my life. But what a rush. None of my story is fabricated or exaggerated. Of course, you have to take my word for that, oh and I do have a few photos.

My Story

After an unhappy childhood and a failed teenage marriage, my thoughts were always one of wanderlust. I wanted to see the world one country at a time. So in the summer of 1978 I began to do just that. Starting with Greece, I worked as a nanny then as a maid in a hotel in Athens. The next summer I got a job with Grecian Holidays which allowed me to visit just about all of the Greek islands, Most of Europe was covered over the next few years, ending with Israel, Egypt and Turkey. 1990 was the year I made a decision that would later change my life.

I had endured an entire year in England, don't get me wrong I love England in the summer, even with the little bit of sun we actually see. However, the winters are another story. It was January and I was really depressed. I hated my job working for a free newspaper as a receptionist and my love life was non-existent. I had kept in contact with some crazy Aussie girls that I had met on the Greek island of Crete, and they had begged me to pay them a visit. However, I was reluctant to do that because they were lunatics, wearing me out with their relentless energy and excessive drinking. But what the hell, I had always wanted to visit Australia. I wrote to them and disappointment came in the form of them turning up on my doorstep, all eager to carry on the party they had created in Crete. Norwich was of course way too quiet for these party animals and they headed off to London, without me, my choice. So here I was back to Square One.

However, a girl in my office had endured my whining for weeks and came to my rescue with an idea. She had worked in California as a nanny, and had kept in contact with her employers. She said that if I wanted, she could get me a nanny job in Los Angeles. I went home that night and thought about the idea. America, very daunting, but on the other hand very exciting. Could I do this? Could I travel to the other side of the world alone? They did of course speak English, that had to be a plus, and after watching so many movies I kind of felt I knew the place. So I threw caution to the wind and the next day I told Sarah to contact her friend. It was only a couple of days later when my phone rang, and a lady with an American accent was asking to speak to me. Everything was happening so fast, and panic set in as I realised she was offering me a job. I told her yes, and after hanging up, sat for the longest time letting it all sink in. After telling Sarah my good news, I realised I had a home to rent out, a car to sell and a month's notice to give at work.

The next four weeks just flew by and I didn't have time to think about the crazy decision I had made. Everything came together with a hitch, which I took as a good omen. My destiny, to live and work in America!

So here I was sitting on a plane bound for Los Angeles, California. I found myself thinking about the movie *Pretty Woman*. I had just watched it and fantasised about finding my knight in shining armour in the form of Richard Gere. The glamour of Beverley Hills, the not so glamourous Hollywood. Could that happen to me, the Knight part of course, not being a hooker. The fasten seat belt sign had come on and looking down all I could see were freeways, and had everyone got a swimming pool in their garden? Well there was no turning back now, this was it. My stomach was now in knots. I was so nervous thinking of the different scenarios I could now face. What if she wasn't at the gate to pick me up. Maybe they wouldn't let me in the country without a six-month visa. I only had a visitor's visa. What if she wasn't the nice lady on the phone and had sent a gangster who wanted me to work as a prostitute. Ok so I watched way too many movies.

Customs took forever and all I could think of, was that this lady had either left the airport out of sheer boredom, or assuming I hadn't made the fight. So many people were holding up cards with names on them, none of them were mine. Then I remembered I had sent a photo to my new employer so she knew who to look out for. Then I saw a nice lady with a friendly smiling face heading straight for me.

I had been correct about how lovely this lady was, she was warm and friendly and put me at ease immediately.

I don't remember much about the car journey to their home, I was so tired, but I do remember pulling up in the drive and seeing what looked like a gingerbread house out of a Walt Disney movie. In the light of day I realised I hadn't dreamt that, it really did resemble a gingerbread house.

Jet lagged and tired, she showed me straight to room and said we would talk in the morning. I woke quite early and very disoriented. But very anxious to meet this family. Lesley being such a sweet lady was honest with me from the word go. Her previous nanny hadn't worked her notice and with both parents working, they needed immediate child care, so they had no choice but to hire a replacement nanny. They knew I had rented my home, sold my car, and left my job. Having made all these life changing decisions with the understanding I had a job, left them feeling really sorry. These were truly lovely people, because they didn't have to take responsibility for what was clearly their previous nanny's fault. They explained that they had several friends that needed nannies and failing that, they would advertise in the LA Times. Wow, what an amazing family

Lesley already had someone in mind, a male colleague at work had problems keeping a nanny and needed one a.s.a.p. I suppose the part where he said he had problems keeping a nanny should have rung alarm bells in our ears. Anyway, he wanted someone to take care of the children all week, Monday through Friday. Then Lesley said at weekends I could spend time at their home relaxing and doing occasional babysitting. Sounded great.

This new family picked me up on the Sunday night ready for Monday morning. Their home was in the Valley, which was a little disappointing as I knew the Valley had a reputation for being very hot in the summer and I would be away from Beverley Hills and the shops. Of course they were financially out of my league, but I could window shop. I soon understood why they couldn't keep a nanny. The husband was ok, the wife however I think you could only describe as a strange, neurotic, psycho bitch. In England the children would be candidates for child abuse. The girl had been overfed from birth and weighed a ton. The boy was five years old and still wore nappies. At first I thought he must have a medical problem, ok if he just wet himself, but doing a crap at that age was truly disgusting and also a little sad. So I had two lots of baby nappies to change, even though one was a small child, and doing all the basic things for the girl was a chore because she weighed so much. My first week was a nightmare and it was such a relief to go to Lesley's for the weekend. Hello lady, we have something in England, it's called potty training.

I was pretty quiet all weekend, not wanting to make a complaint to Lesley about her work colleague, because it would have been really rude after all she had done for me. I walked into Beverley Hills and looked around for any employment agency. Before leaving England, Sarah had given me the name and address of one just in case I needed it. Hell I did need it. I registered with them and they said they did have a vacancy right now, but did I have a California Driver's Licence, as it was essential for the job. I was going to lie, especially as upon snooping at the paperwork I saw the name on the request for a nanny was Robin Williams. I decided not to take the chance but go away and somehow get my licence, and come back when I had it.

Even though I thought I had hidden my stress about the family from Lesley, she had noticed how unhappy I was. So on the Monday at work she asked around the office, in an attempt to get any feedback on the family. To her horror, her colleagues told her she'd done a terrible thing sending me there, that the wife was crazy and the children simply revolting.

Lesley felt really bad and on picking me up from there the next weekend, apologised and told me I didn't have to go back. What a relief that was. Still I was back to square one, no job and running out of money. Of course I didn't account for Lesley already having a game plan. She had placed an advert in the *LA Times*. English Nanny looking for live-in work. The response was overwhelming, the phone rang off the hook, guess it's a Mary Poppins thing. We tried to cram in as many interviews as possible. Lesley had to go into work so walking, cycling or the bus were my only options. I was very surprised and a little disturbed by the amount of weirdos and perverts who answered the ad. Men who needed a nanny but didn't actually have children, Yuk!! Lesley then told me that I needed my California driving licence, it was essential that I had it when going for jobs. She took me to the D.M.V. for my written test, no problems passing that. Then out for a drive to get me used to driving on the right side of the road.

After a morning of one interview after another, exhausted, hot and tired, I returned home and was greeted by a very excited Lesley.

While I was out she'd had a call from a lady in Bel Air, asking me to attend an interview that very afternoon. Lesley was adamant that I went for this interview, as everyone who lived in Bel Air was rich.

I barely had time to wash, eat and change, when I was running out of the door to have an interview with God knows who! Scared again for the second time in a couple of weeks. A long bus journey and a walk in the heat and I was there. Oh yes, these people were rich alright, I found myself standing in front of some very large electric gates. After pressing the security button and announcing who I was, they slowly drew back, revealing a beautiful, very large white house.

A maid answered the door and showed me into a room which was full of ladies. I wasn't the only person being interviewed for this job and I realised that with no experience or references, I had no chance of getting it. It was like United Nations in there, every ethnic group imaginable and I was sure these women had way more experience than I had. We all sat waiting for quite some time. Then the front door burst open and this very attractive, casually dressed woman apologised for keeping everyone waiting, and ran upstairs. I turned to the girl beside me and asked how long she had been waiting, and she told me over an hour, crikey, I thought, how rude was this woman keeping everyone waiting all this time. She then started the interviews and went through them with lightning speed. In and out with their feet barely touching the ground.

I'd travelled quite a way to attend this interview and imagined some of these ladies had travelled even further. So how rude was this lady, not giving them a decent amount of time. I was sure I'd be dismissed in the same way and I started to think about what I was going to say to her to express my disgust and the rude way she conducted herself. I later found out that the reason she had taken very little time with the others was because she had already made her decision to hire me, the English person.

I was shown around the house and then taken to the garden, where there were two girls playing. They were both very pretty and blonde like their mother. A gentleman stood there in a suit, looked like he'd just come from an office, he was holding a small boy in his arms, also blonde and cute. The man asked me to take the little boy and I held out my arms, he came to me without any fuss at all, much to the surprise of his parents. Apparently he didn't usually take too well to strangers. I guessed by their delight that this was the little fellow I'd be taking care of. My interview was over, I was thanked and told I'd be receiving a call later on that day.

It took me a while to get back to Lesley's and her smiling face on my arrival, told me that she had already heard from them and had some good news for me. I had instructions to go the husband's office on the Monday and I'd meet with his secretary, who would let me know what my duties would be, salary, start date, etc.

Monday came and I was very nervous. Since arriving in Los Angeles I had solely relied on Lesley, and this time I was on my own, there was no going back. Lesley had done so much for me, I couldn't let her down. I messed up big time finding the office. After looking on a map, I had decided that getting on a bus and getting off at Fairfax and Santa Monta Boulevard was going to bring me very close to the office, oh how wrong was I. Not knowing that Santa Monica goes all the way from one side of Los Angeles and down to the beach was my down fall. Getting off the bus left me with several miles of walking. That wasn't my only big mistake; I had purchased some new shoes especially for my interview. So after about two miles of the five-mile hike, I had some really nice blisters on my heels. When I finally reached the address I'd been given, the blisters had turned into nice bloody gaping sores. What a fantastic fashion statement, white shoes with a stream of blood cascading down the heel. The office building was of course really posh which made me even more conscious of the state of my footwear.

The office I needed was on the ninth floor, of course it was. Oh what joy, still not quite at my destination. All I needed, a bit more pain and more blood that was now filling my shoes, yeah!

I opened the door to the office and was immediately welcomed by a lady with a lovely friendly smile, Wendy. She was Mr Hilton's personal secretary and soon made me feel at ease. I didn't know at the time that this lovely lady would become my rock in some very stormy seas. She got straight down to business. This was no ordinary family, they were the Hiltons, Yes, the hotel chain Hiltons. I didn't want to show my ignorance but I wasn't even aware that Hiltons were American.

As their hotels were all over England, I had wrongly assumed they were English. She went on to tell me firstly all about the family then what was expected of me. I was really relieved that I was not being employed as a nanny, but as a personal assistant to Mrs Hilton. Wendy had been juggling both jobs of being assistant to both Mr & Mrs H. Mr Hilton had a very successful real estate business, he wasn't involved in his father's hotel business. So he had suggested that Mrs H have her own personal assistant.

Wendy then went on to tell me about my other responsibilities which included overseeing the staff at the house and making sure everything in the house ran smoothly. All good news to me. She went on to explain that the Hilton's had planned a three-week vacation to Europe. They would need me to play the role of nanny to young Barron just for that period of time. His nanny being Hispanic, could not leave the United States as she didn't have the relevant papers to return. Wendy had been their first choice but they needed her to oversee Mr Hilton's business while they were away. Oh well, I'd be travelling round Europe, visiting Paris and Italy, staying at the very best hotels and dining at the best restaurants. Not too shabby.

I backed out of the office trying to talk to Wendy and hide the blood stains that were now streaks down the back of my shoes. I limped to the bus stop and managed to get off at the right stop this time. Of course, this was too little too late to save my shoes from having to be thrown. Packed and heels plastered up, I set off to me new life in Bel Air. How cool was that?

Have to say I was a bit disappointed with my room. Very small and I had a tiny window, which made it feel dark and a little damp. Hey ho, at least I had my own room and privacy, so not fazed at all. I went upstairs to the kitchen to meet the staff, they were not at all friendly and pretended not to speak English.

Mrs H was out shopping so I made a decision to wander round the rest of the house, to get my bearings. The lounge was full of sterling silver picture frames, filled with photographs of rich and famous people. Photos of Michael Jackson, Kenny Rogers, Tom Hanks and even Ronald and Nancy Reagan, to name but a few. I was quite shocked that they knew such famous people and intrigued as to whether I would ever get to meet any of these celebrities. Imagining how cool that would be, mouth opened, suddenly the door flung open and made me jump. In ran the two pretty blonde girls I'd previously met in the garden. They did not stop to say hello. First impressions of these two, they had no manners. I was still gawping at the photos when Mrs H came in. I was a little embarrassed not knowing if it was appropriate for me to wander around their home like that. She asked me if the girls were home and when I told her they were, she asked if I would go introduce myself to them and see if they needed any help with their homework. Pleased I had something to do, I went upstairs.

Nicky, the youngest, seven years old was very nice and eagerly accepted my help with her homework. Her sister however was not so friendly, just nine years old and was already a proper little princess. Paris Hilton came across as a spoilt, precocious, little daddy's girl, he'd already nicknamed her Star and she had already made the decision that she was never going to work for a living, that she was rich and would always have people take care of her every whim. I remember once suggesting that she make her own bed, she replied, that's what maids are for. I told her that when she grows up she might not have a maid. She burst into laughter and said "Of course I'll have a maid". Thinking back now to the first time I met Paris, my impression was that this young lady will fall flat on her face, if she thinks she won't need a job or at least some education. Guess I was wrong there.

It would soon be vacation time. Mrs H told me to get to know young Barron, and obviously get him to like me. I would be his carer for the duration of the trip. Mimi, his current nanny, Hispanic and a child herself, I guessed around seventeen years, was none too pleased about the situation and got in my way at every opportunity. Fortunately, in spite of her jealousy and interferences, I managed to get the boy to really like me. So my next task was persuading Mimi that I was not trying to take Barron or her job away from her. Once I had convinced her that I had no intentions of doing either, we got on really well.

During the time I worked for the Hiltons, many a disastrous event occurred. Some were very funny, others I can honestly say were actually life threatening. So here is my first encounter.

The children had been playing over at their grandparents home all day, playing with a cousin who was visiting, Nicky had returned home earlier alone and told me that Paris was having a sleepover. Mr and Mrs H had gone out to dinner as they did most evenings. The phone range and it was Paris in hysterics screaming that she wanted to come home. I told her that there was no one to drive and get her as her parents were out.

She was yelling about there being a ghost at her grandparent's home and that she was too scared to sleep there. I told her that there were no such things as ghosts. I had no way of picking her up having no transport and I hung up. I could never have guessed what she would do next, she rang every restaurant her parents ever dined at and tracked them down. Paris was not used to people saying no to her and she had no intentions of starting with me. When I received the call from them telling me to go and pick her up, I was so shocked that they had given in to this spoilt brat. I reminded them that although I had a British driving licence, I had not taken my California licence or driven on the right side of the road before. This didn't seem to matter to them, Paris wanted to come home and what Paris wanted …..

The Hiltons had gone to dinner in the Bentley so the only other car was a Range Rover, a top of the range $50K Range Rover. Take Nicky with you for directions, they had said, great let's not only kill myself but your daughters as well. Nicky had no idea of the way in the dark, so what should have been a ten-minute drive took us nearly thirty minutes.

Nicky jumped out of the car and rang the buzzer on the security gate telling whoever answered to open the gates for us. The gates drew back and she got back into the Range Rover. Shock, horror, I was only halfway through the gates when they started to close, not at a nice slow pace either so I put my foot down. These suckers close so fast that only hitting the sides of this really expensive car slowed them down. It was then I noticed a crazy lady waving her arms and shouting. It seemed like she was blaming me for what was happening to the Hilton's $50K car. The gates stopped closing but we couldn't get out. When the woman finally reached us, she said she had called the Bel Air patrol who would most certainly help us. Paris was smiling and I wanted to slap her stupid face, if she hadn't called her parents and screamed and sulked for me to come and get her none of this would have happened.

When we arrived back home, the girls jumped out of the car both laughing. I however was shocked and horrified. I thought I had no alternative but to hand in my resignation. Let's face it, I'd damaged a very expensive vehicle. I couldn't imagine them wanting to employ me after that. I put the letter in their room, explaining just what had happened, and then I went straight to bed. I heard them come in and knew that they would go straight upstairs. The phone in my room rang and I was very nervous. Mrs H was laughing on the other end, and said not to worry. Apparently the same gates had closed on Mr H's brother's Porsche just a week before. What a relief, I wasn't going to be jobless and homeless.

Feeling a little guilty then about the way I had been to Paris and Nicky, I went up to their rooms to check they were alright and ask Paris about this so-called ghost that she had been so scared of. She told me that this ghost had haunted the Hilton mansion for years, and that everyone had seen it at some time. The ghost was one of a small girl who had been run over and killed on the drive many years ago. The cousin had been teasing Paris that it was in the house and in their bedroom that night and she could see her. I told her it was silly, and that there were no such things as ghosts. Well, that's what I told her. I did in fact believe in them and had thought I had a ghost residing in a property I once lived in. Paris then ranted on about it being the ghost that had closed the gates on the Range Rover. Maybe she had a point.

In the morning I went outside to peruse the damage to the Range Rover and much to my amazement and relief it really wasn't that bad. The cloud that had hung above my head last night had gone and I was ready to face the day ahead, or was I. Who knew this day would bring sheer bedlam into my life. To say things seemed really manic this morning was an understatement.

As a rule, Mrs H didn't get out of her pit until late morning, and here she was up and about and giving out orders right, left and centre. I asked her what was going on and she apologised for not letting me know sooner. Apparently today Mrs H and her girls were modelling in a charity show at the Regent Beverly Wilshire Hotel. We all bundled into the car and headed for Beverly Hills. First on the agenda was hair. Mrs H went to José Ebers Beverly Hills, hairdresser to the stars. The girls went to a children's hair salon just over the road. I had been given $200 for both girls and they were only having trims and blow-dries. The cost seemed a tad expensive to me, but after watching these poor hairstylists trying to work with these precocious little brats, I could see they really earned their money.

They wouldn't sit still, and complained about the way their hair was being blown dry. Screaming if they thought too much hair was being cut off. Paris had a big strop and decided she wasn't having anything done to her hair, and I had to remind her that she was about to be a model in a charity event, and that this was her mother's wish. She finally caved. I can't remember the movie but it reminded me of a girl who said in a very precocious way, I'm going to scream and scream until I'm sick. Being in the presence of such rude and bad-mannered children embarrassed me so much, I could have thrown up. I began to wonder if I truly was cut out to deal with the spawn of the rich and famous. We hadn't even left the salon and to my horror, Paris was brushing her hair out and was trying to restyle it to her liking. Not only had she just wasted time and money, but I was thinking about Mrs H and how she would react to Paris looking like she'd been dragged through a hedge backwards. Then I remembered that Paris very rarely washed her hair, so at the very least, it was clean hair. I was right her mum didn't even notice she'd combed the style out. It looked lighter and shinier, just because it was clean.

We had more running about to do before we arrived at the event and in true Hilton style, we arrived late. The Beverly Wilshire Hotel, how grand. This was the very hotel that Julia Roberts and Richard Gere had stayed, in the movie *Pretty Woman*. It did seem grander in real life and the bench she had perched on outside did not exist, obviously just a prop.

We rushed back stage to get ready. Of course most of the ladies were ready, we were late as usual so everything was a rush. The changing room was full of half-naked beautiful women, who didn't care about showing off their bodies. Hell, if I looked like that naked I'd probably be happy to show off my body. I was a little naïve then and hadn't been there long enough to know that these women bought cosmetic surgery in the same way us mere mortals bought make-up. Of course I did wonder why most of the women had large boobs and why the older women's boobs were so perky.

Mrs H had her own dress changes to worry about so left me to deal with Paris and Nicky, fortunately they had only one walk to do. Dressed in matching pretty pink silk dresses, they did manage the walk with some sign of finesse. Well Paris did anyway, she strutted her little butt down that runway, posing and acting with confidence, being the Star that daddy had nicknamed her. Backstage I met a few of the ladies participating in the charity. A lady called Pia Zadora, I'd never heard of her, but apparently she was famous in America for her singing. Certainly a big unknown in England.

Then I met the wide of Mark Hughes, Suzan. Mark was the founder and owner of Herbalife, a multi-million dollar company that I had heard of. They sold herbal and slimming products and had outlets all over the world. I had even worked for them once on a part-time basis for a short time in England.

Suzan was very petite, with huge breasts that were obviously not home grown, and she was wearing five-inch heels. Her little frame, huge boobs and high heels made her look top heavy, and you felt you might need to hold out your hands to catch her, feeling she might topple over at any moment. I met Mark later and seeing that he was over six-foot tall, I realised that this was the reason this little lady wore such high shoes. She was pretty and very sweet, but somewhat of a Barbie doll. Ok I had only just met this couple, but first impressions, they were so mismatched. He was tall, dark and very handsome and appeared very well educated. Suzan not so much, let's just say bleached blonde, short, pretty and appeared to be not so bright. Of course, she had managed to snag a millionaire husband so not too dumb, right. So looking around I guessed most of these women were professional models and as I wasn't a regular subscriber to Vogue magazine, or had ever purchased said magazine, I had no clue who they were.

When the girls were finished, we all went to the front where the Hiltons had a table reserved. Mimi was there with Barron and was still being unfriendly. There were free goodie bags on the table filled with great gifts and we both noticed that people were leaving and not taking the bags with them. Mimi had already worked out that the goodies in the bags were really quite nice, so she had snagged a couple, I followed suit, realising what was crap to these people was pretty good to Mimi and I. Grabbing some more on our way out and laughing together helped break the ice between us a little. So what had been a really shitty start to the day had turned out to be fun. So maybe I could handle working for these people after all. Hell I guess I could.

Vacation time had arrived and the girls had been given strict instructions from their parents, to pack light, Mr H asked me to check that these instructions had been adhered to. Shock, horror, the girls had packed all but the kitchen sink. Two bags each and no toys were the instructions. Well, Miss Paris wasn't going to be told by me what she could and couldn't take on her vacation. I opened the bags and started to throw out toys and winter clothes, as I unpacked, she repacked. Nicky had done as she was told and removed all toys and winter clothes, but this girl was going to be a big pain in my butt. After fighting with her for a while I decided to go down to tell her father and try to get to my room to pack my own things. It was no surprise to me that he had given in to his little princess and she still had four bags to her sister's two. It was the look of contempt she gave me for getting her own way, that had been the most annoying. I did however get my own back. When she went to say goodbye to her numerous pets, I took out her toys and winter clothes and she finished up with three bags. On packing my things, I realised that I hadn't got the kind of attire that would be appropriate for fine restaurants and hotels, even if I was only the help, I still needed to look like I fitted in these places, so I packed light, deciding to buy a whole new wardrobe when I got there.

I understood Mr H's anxiety when the maids started to bring down their luggage. Mrs H had more than a dozen bags all full to the brim and all Louis Vuitton. Enough clothes for a year's vacation and it was obvious that she would buy lots more in Europe. So there it was all, dozens of bags and Mr H's golf clubs, God only knows why he decided to lug them along. Then he told me that one of my jobs was to keep count of the bags on our trip, so none got left behind anywhere. Oh what joy. Paris had three and Nicky's two made five, plus the Hilton's twelve, and my two totalled nineteen, then I decided to count the golf clubs as a bag, so twenty.

Wendy, Mr H's secretary, burst through the door, in a huge panic, asking why we hadn't left for the airport yet. I hadn't known this family long but had already worked out that they all did everything at their own pace. I'd doubt they'd rush for water if their arse was on fire. There was a limo outside and driver told me he'd already been waiting over an hour. Wendy was getting frustrated and annoyed, and told me it was her responsibility to make sure we got the flight, not too much pressure there then. There was a major point overlooked, how the hell were we and all the luggage going to fit in the limo? A quick decision had to be made if we were to make our flight.

Bags were lugged downstairs by the maids, they had been counted by me. Most of the luggage and Mr and Mrs H were piled into the limo and Wendy took the overspill in her car. She had called a taxi to come and pick us up a.s.a.p. It arrived very quickly, and we got to the airport around the same time as the limo. From then on everything was just madness. One big rush. Wendy gave me a big hug and wished me luck, I thought that was strange, here I was about to go on the vacation of a lifetime to Europe, staying at the best hotels and eating at the best restaurants. Not too shabby. Wendy had been working for the Hiltons for a lot of years and knew that I not only needed luck, but a few prayers wouldn't go amiss.

Of course, Mr H and Mrs H had seats in first class, we mere mortals had seats in coach. This wouldn't have been too bad if they had booked me in a seat with a cot in front to put Barron. Great, nowhere for him to sleep other than on my lap. I wasn't going to get any sleep then!

We had been sitting for quite some time, when finally an explanation came from the captain, The automatic refuelling system had broken down, and we were being refuelled manually. Great, the girls were playing running up and down the aisles. The flight attendants were constantly telling them to sit down. Barron was whining for his baba, which was his name for his bottle. To keep him quiet of course I gave in, this decision had consequences, I had to keep changing his nappy. This all went on for two hours. By the time we took off, I was already pissed off. The eleven-hour flight was no better, the girls didn't settle and I got no peace or sleep. The flight attendants kept complaining to me about the girl's behaviour. So eleven hours later, no sleep and fully exhausted, we finally arrive at Heathrow Airport. What a great start to the vacation. A vacation that I would later describe, as the vacation from hell.

Hello England, funny it seems like I never left you. Well it had only been two months. This was now June, so at least we arrived into glorious sunshine. There was a limo waiting for us, sent from the family hotel. Of course there was not enough room for us all and the luggage, so guess who had to schlep all the luggage into taxis and go on behind.

The Conrad Hilton was a fairly new hotel, I witnessed some serious butt kissing on the way in, from staff. You would think royalty had arrived rather than just the owner's son and his family.

The girls and I had adjoining rooms, a cot in mine for young Barron. Mr and Mr H were along the corridor, I guessed to get some privacy, hell they had very little at home.

I was barely settled in when Paris came bursting through my door. Missing two of her bags, she accused me of not doing my job. This of course being the job her father had given me, counting bags. I told her that I had counted them correctly and that she was missing two bags because they had been unpacked at home. The tantrum I then observed was astonishing, crying and screaming in temper. Oh what joy, she was just as precocious here as at home.

Expecting to get some well needed sleep that night was just a dream. A nightmare in reality. Mimi being a child herself had let Barron develop some really bad habits. These of course were not evident to me in L.A. as these were bedtime habits. I discovered that he cried every two hours in the night for what he called his baba. This was his bottle, which she filled with juice. To save her getting in and out of bed all night she let him sleep in her bed, and filled several bottles with his juice. Life made easier for her, but shit for me. And of course, everyone knows that what goes in must come out, so the amount of fluid intake this boy had on a nightly basis meant his nappies overflowed with pee, soaking him and more importantly, the bed I was sharing with him. This isn't a habit you can correct in days or weeks, so I had to go along with it, if only to get some sleep. Hey it did give me pleasure to think I was giving him back to her in a few weeks, in the same damaged state she'd given him to me.

Waking up to a wet patch in the morning was both uncomfortable and embarrassing. I didn't want the maid to think I had wet the bed, so I smoothed out the covers on his cot and punched dents into both pillows. Still; not convinced that the maid would know it wasn't me wetting the bed, I waited in the room for them to arrive so I could explain what the problem was, or rather who the problem was. She was really sweet and said she'd change the sheets daily for me and explain to the other maids that it wasn't me with the waterworks problem.

It was getting near to lunchtime, the girls were getting restless and neither parent had come over to tell us the plans for the day. Guess they were having a nice lie-in, what I wouldn't give for the same luxury. When Mr H finally came over to our room, he explained that entertaining the girls was going to be my job. He wanted me to show the girls all the sights of London. A limo would pick us up and take us anywhere I suggested, and would spend the entire day with us. He gave me £200 and said it was spending money for food etc. Ok, so what were we going to do all day?

Of course, they had made plans to spend the day at Wimbledon watching the tennis. So this was the reality, these guys had brought their children with them on holiday but had absolutely no intentions of actually spending any amount of time with them. I couldn't decide if this was sad, tragic, or both.

There were still nine of the ten London vacation days left, and I wondered how on earth I was going to keep these spoilt brats amused for this length of time. They were not going to be easy. I did ask the girls if there was anything they thought they might like to do. They had no clue, so I made some suggestions. They had no interest in visiting any old buildings, "their words". They had no interest in art, culture or history so what the hell was left? This was going to be a long, long nine days. I made the mistake of taking them to the Tower of London and a bigger mistake telling the driver it was ok to pick us up in two hours. The girls were bored after about then minutes and constantly complained and whined. Shit, this was just day one.

Everyone was hungry by now and I had been given a good amount of pocket money for us all to have a really nice lunch. Now these girls had been taught no manners, that included table manners. I didn't care when we were in America because table manners didn't seem to be an essential part of American life. I however had a whole different upbringing and good manners played a big part in my life. So I figured wherever I took them, they would embarrass me. So where did table manners not matter? Yeah! When the girls suggested McDonalds I was so relieved, it didn't matter to me how they behaved in there. I wouldn't even care if people thought they were my children.

The poor limo driver's face when he dropped us off. I did give him a nice tip, hey, I had lots of money left over and his limo needed some serious cleaning up inside.

So this day had gone ok, but we still had another eight to go and I was struggling to think of somewhere that would amuse them for an entire day. I hoped the limo driver had some ideas in the morning. Mr and Mrs H didn't come back to the hotel until really late as they dined out. They did ring and tell me to order the girls, myself and Barron something off the hotel menu. So that was ok. I was so tired that night I actually slept ok. In spite of a peeing toddler in my bed.

When the limo came the next day, I asked the driver if he had any suggestions for the day's excursion, explaining how difficult it was to amuse these obnoxious children. He suggested we take them to Leicester Square and then Piccadilly Circus. I did think it an odd decision, but he was spot on. Who knew these children would love feeding the pigeons. I bought them bags of seed from the vendor and they were mesmerised by how tame they were, the birds not the children. They were entertained for hours. They just loved the birds that were allowing them to feed from their hands. They had never experienced tame birds that would sit on your shoulder, hand and even your head. Of course Paris was horrified when one pigeon decided to poo on her. She was screaming at me to wipe it off and all I could do was laugh. She sulked all the way back to the hotel and couldn't wait to tell her dad how mean I was. He found it just as amusing as me, so she had no luck there. Anyway, her parents were heading out of the hotel, they had dinner reservations with friends again and didn't want to hear about Paris's nonsense.

Another day in paradise with these wonderful children, "hint of sarcasm". We had a different driver today and his suggestion was the Zoo. That turned out to be another great idea. Not only did the girls have a great day, I actually had a fun day too. There was so much to do and I heard no whining. Pleasure to my ears. I should have realised, both girls had so many pets at home, they obviously loved animals and birds. I couldn't thank the driver enough.

I guessed the driver was weighing me up. It was obvious he was a little reserved in how much he told me. Once he felt secure enough that I wouldn't pass on anything he said onto the Hiltons, he told me some gossip. Apparently the drivers would draw straws in the morning, the shortest straw being the loser, and would have the Hilton assignment for the day. Even after receiving a good tip, none of the drivers wanted the assignment. Wrecking the inside of the limo and the rude way they were spoken to, no amount of money covered that.

A couple of days later I got the same driver, After we had joked about him getting the short straw again, he asked me how I coped with such rude and obnoxious children, I told him how I'd only been working for them a few weeks prior to the vacation, so I had no idea they were going to be such hard work.

I told him, he sighed, and said he would pray for me. His look of sympathy reminded me of the look on Wendy's face when she wished me good luck at the airport. Wendy had worked for them for a lot of years, so I guessed she had probably been on one of these trips before and knew exactly what I was about to ensure. I hoped she was praying for me too. The more the merrier, maybe it would help me to avoid having a nervous breakdown in the near future.

Unlike most people's jobs, mine didn't finish at 6 o'clock. I had the evenings to ensure too. The Hiltons were too sharp for that, they knew that fine restaurants in England were not going to accept their children's bad manners, the other diners would complain. Even if they weren't asked to leave, I'm sure they would never be able to return. I pictured them trying to book another night and on hearing the name Hilton, being told "Sorry, we are full this evening". So to save everyone from an embarrassing episode, the Hiltons ate out alone or with friends. I was ok with that.

However room service was limited and as the girls and I had spent the day eating junk food, I really wanted them to eat something more nutritious for dinner. If I ordered for them, the food didn't get eaten so I gave in and let them order for themselves, I just dealt with Barron's meal. Great, he really only ever wanted to eat Spaghetti Bolognese.

Shit, would he pick a messier food? I can't describe the mess that occurred. His face was covered in sauce, as were his clothes, the high chair and all the surrounding area. I soon realised that putting down toilet paper on the carpet was the only way I could save it from extreme staining.

The Conrad Hilton Hotel.
Barron loved his spaghetti, the carpet not so much.

Taking care of Barron was easy, apart from his babas and nappies he really wasn't any trouble. The girls had wrecked their room and then bored to tears and high on a sugar rush, would run amok around the hotel. I didn't care, if it meant peace and quiet for me.

I knew the hotel would make sure they came to no harm, let's face it their jobs depended on it. The manager called up to the room nightly. Always complaining that the girls were wrecking his hotel. They loved to play at the reception desk, pretending to be receptionists. He was having a nightmare, because they were wiping out vital information on the computer. I said the same thing every night, "Just send them up to me". Having Barron to take care of was my excuse for not coming down to get them.

None of the staff dared to get angry with the girls. These were the grandchildren of the owner. The man that paid their wages. I guess I should have been more responsible for these girls, but I looked at it this way. They were monsters, way before the family employed me. I hadn't been involved in their upbringing. I hadn't made them rude and bad mannered. Someone else had done a good job of that. So why should I feel responsible for them wrecking their grandfather's hotel.

They would come back to their room and wait a little before they went back down again. I did have a little sympathy for them as there was nothing for them to do in their room. They got bored, stir crazy, and they had parents who obviously didn't give a shit about them. They decided that returning to reception was probably a bad idea, so they felt the kitchen might just be more welcoming. It wasn't of course. They soon called up and told me the girls were messing up the kitchen. Removing data from the front desk was one thing, the fear of them burning down the hotel was another. This time I put Barron in the stroller and rushed down to get the girls. The staff were so pleased to see me.

I wanted to catch Mr Hilton before he went off for the day, I needed him to know how tired I was and needed a day off. Big surprise, he announced they were both going off to Ireland for a couple of days with Michael Caine. What the flip, when were they going to tell me? Oh I guess they just did. I was even more confused. Exactly why had they brought the children on this vacation. After dropping this bombshell on me, I was promised a day off on their return. He gave me £400 expenses and left.

I couldn't stand another day of garbage food and feeding bloody birds. I called down to room service and had them make up a lovely packed lunch and I told the driver to take us to Whipsnade Safari Park.

Whipsnade Safari Park. A more successful day out in London. Paris and Barron.

This turned out to be a huge success, a nice day was had by all. Yeah! Not wanting to go back to the hotel just yet I had the driver take us to another park, where the girls could enjoy their favourite pastime, feeding the birds. I bought several bags of seed and didn't notice that Nicky had placed one of her bags on Barron's lap. There was a lovely Kodak moment with the girls standing in front of some beautiful swans. Then I turned round to check on Barron and he had disappeared under a mound of pigeons. There was a faint scream and the girls started laughing, the poor little chap was buried as the flying rats pecked at the now ripped bag on his lap. It did look funny so I didn't tell the girls off for laughing, hell it was hard for me not to laugh.

I quickly shooed the birds away and hugged him. Poor Barron was traumatised and I couldn't help but wonder if he would grow up having an irrational fear of birds when he got older and would never understand why. The next time we went to Piccadilly Circus he made it quite clear that he was having nothing to do with them, by screaming at the top of his lungs, bless him.

The Hiltons were back from their trip to Ireland. It was time for me to have a well-earned day off. I was smiling to myself, imagining them coping an entire day with the girls and Barron.

I however had a great day. I shopped with the three weeks wages I was given. I wanted nice clothes for Italy, even if it was going to be like London, me and the girls fending for ourselves. I wanted to be dressed nicely in such a beautiful country. Ah freedom! I had a nice lunch in a nice restaurant. That smile sprang back on my face, as I wondered how they were coping with their brood. I must have looked like a crazy person smiling away to myself. Oh well this was all short lived, I had hoped for a day and a night of freedom but a day is not twenty-four hours to these people. They couldn't wait to drop off the kids and get the hell out to another nice restaurant. Before they left Mrs H actually told me a funny story. Well she thought it was funny, I thought it sad. They had taken the children shopping for the day. Bet they enjoyed that. NOT. Anyway, Mrs H was entering Cartier, Barron in her arms. The security man outside was shaking his head, indicating that she couldn't enter the store. Because he was looking at Barron, she assumed that he was saying children were not allowed in the store, thinking it strange but accepting this had to be a rule, she handed Barron over to Paris so she could enter alone. Paris however was disgusted and handed him straight back, indicating that the poor boy had poop all down his legs. Poor Barron hadn't been changed all day, his mum hadn't even thought about it. She was crying with laughter telling me the story, I tried to look amused but quite honestly, I was horrified and saddened, So off they went to dinner and I ordered from room service yet again. The girls went off to annoy the hotel staff and I tried to have a nap, knowing that I was probably in for another disturbed night's sleep.

The morning was a big shock, this was going to be a second day they spent with the kids, this time with me in tow. I thought about it and realised the girls probably grassed me up about not visiting interesting places. This was made evident when we visited only touristy places. Bet they didn't tell their dad that I tried to take them and they had refused to stop whining. Wanting only to feed stupid birds.

Outside Buckingham Palace.
L-R Kathy, Paris, Nicky and me.

So we went to Buckingham Palace, took a few photographs and then headed to Westminster Abbey. The girls looked so bored. Of course Mrs H hadn't had her daily shopping fix so Knightsbridge was our next stop. Home of designer shops and Harrods. It had started to rain pretty hard and our limo driver held an umbrella over everyone's heads as they dashed for shelter. As he went to hold it over my head, I said it's ok, I'm no one. His reply to me was "everyone is someone". Simple words but very poignant. His words have always stayed with me.

Family shopping day out. I'm at the front of the limo looking confused.

The ten days in London were coming to an end along with my patience. Getting the girls things packed was a nightmare, they had strewn their clothes all over the floor, everything was creased and/or dirty. As for me being in charge of counting bags; that was a joke. Yes, myself and the girls had the same quantity we had started with, but one of our party had doubled their capacity. Yes, Mrs H had shopped each and every day of the vacation. What were once fourteen pieces of luggage had now accumulated into twenty pieces.

As we left the hotel it amused me to see the smiling faces of the staff. Their smiles had been forced and false on our arrival, and on our departure they were all smiling with obvious delight. I was really jealous, their nightmare was over and mine had only just begun.

Of course we only just made the flight, we were late as usual and checking in enough luggage for a family of twenty didn't help.

Florence was beautiful, and was only marred by the company I was in. The hotel we stayed in was the best Florence had to offer, the Hotel Excelsior. We were only staying there for four days so there was a lot to see in such a short time.

Galleria Dell'accademia Florence
Statue of David. Oh, and the Hilton family.

I was really surprised to learn that they had hired a tour guide to take us around all the great sights. A great way to learn all about the history of this amazing city.

The guide was a really nice man and his English was perfect. I was horrified that these ignorant people were not listening to a word he said. Instead they talked amongst themselves, I struggled to hear what he was saying, and felt so embarrassed to be associated with these people. He took us to a lovely family-run restaurant and I couldn't wait to tell him that I was just the help and not related to this family in any way, shape or form. He had guessed I wasn't, especially as I was the only person paying any attention to him, and had politely asked questions.

He said he had been doing the job for thirty years and had never witnessed such rudeness. The food was exquisite. Mr H had ordered everything off the menu. Placed in the middle of the table, we could sample every dish. Italian food is my favourite so I was in my element. We went back to the hotel, hot and tired. It was July and the temperature in Italy was much higher than in England.

That night Barron was being a pain, as per usual. I'd had no success weaning him off his babas. I didn't want him to drink an excess of juice in the night. I didn't speak any Italian so had no way of explaining the wet patch in my bed every night. Weird thing was, I must have retained some sort of sense of humour because I wrote in my diary, *travelling round Europe with a millionaire, staying in the best hotels. Only one problem, every night he wets the bed.* So I actually had a lovely time in Florence. I made myself a promise to one day return with someone I actually liked.

A drive to Pisa airport was next on the agenda. From there we would fly to Paris, ooh la la. Of course the baggage count had grown yet again, so two large vans were hired to carry the bags and we all piled into taxis. Shock horror, we were running late. Nothing new there then. I did manage to take a quick picture of the Leaning Tower. When I got it developed it wasn't leaning, not sure how I managed that.

So on to Paris. We needed five large taxis to take the luggage and ourselves to the posh Ritz Hotel. Now totalling twenty pieces, I was in charge of making sure all pieces were taken into the hotel and were taken to the correct rooms. Well this stay was embarrassing from the get go. The children now looked like bums. The girls were not fond of bathing, and their clothes had been flung on the floor for most of this trip. Also Barron's stroller was particularly scruffy, now covered in food stains. I had tried to keep it clean especially after the bird poo and dirty nappy incident in London. Oh well, the Hiltons didn't seem to give a shit so why should I.

Ritz Hotel, Paris.
L-R Nicky, Paris and Barron.

Pool at the Ritz Hotel.
L-R Nicky, me and Barron.

We only stayed in this prestigious hotel for one night. Madam wasn't happy, she didn't like her room and found it really noisy. I'm sure it had a lot to do with our rooms being right next door. The girls were too near her for comfort. So we moved to the Athénée Hotel. I didn't imagine a hotel being posher than the Ritz, but wow! We were right in the heart of Paris, in the midst of some seriously expensive shops. I thought about the serious damage Mrs H could do to Mr H's wallet.

I began to imagine just how many Louis Vuitton bags I'd be counting after this trip. I was once again reminded that Madam had only come to Europe to shop, and again wondered why she had dragged the children along. Not being a shopaholic myself it was difficult for me to understand the thoughts of someone with this addiction. All these shops could be found in Beverly Hills so why travel all this way to shop?

Now we needed a bus to accommodate all the luggage.

Thank heavens there was a travelling fair set up just down the street. Somewhere for me to take the kids, while the parents shopped. They loved the fair and it wasn't easy to drag them away at the end of the day. Heaven forbid they wanted to see any sights. Even a visit to the Eiffel Tower didn't appeal, and it was in spitting distance of our hotel.

Mr Hilton, exhausted from all his wife's shopping.

The Parisians have a reputation amongst us Brits for not being too fond of British tourists. However I had no idea that's nothing to the contempt they have for American tourists. Especially rich and arrogant ones. Mr H had hired a car for the next day, to take us sightseeing, just me and the children of course. The driver looked really pissed off with us before we even started the day. When we stopped to have some lunch, I thought I would find out what his problem was. Once he heard my accent and realised I wasn't a Hilton, he decided to open up to me. Apparently word had got round that Mr H was a really bad tipper, rude and arrogant, so no one wanted to take them anywhere. Word had also got round that they had brats with them. Mr H had called several companies to take us out for the day, and all were "fully booked". Once he realised what the problem was, he cheated and just told them he needed a car for the day to pick up at the Plaza Athénée. No names were given, or mention of children. That's why the driver looked so pissed off when we jumped into his car.

Thankfully our vacation was coming to an end, so the Parisians didn't have to put up with us for much longer. I too was relieved that this nightmare was coming to an end. Back at the hotel, I was no longer concerned about neatly folding the girl's clothes into their suitcases. My main concern was counting the new mound of suitcases we were leaving Europe with. Forty in total. It would have taken a fleet of taxis, to take us and the luggage to the airport, so there was no alternative, I had to go to their room to count the bags there. Of course mine, Barron's and the girls totalled the same as when we left. So adding them both together made forty in total. Mr H reminded me that counting the bags and making sure they were all loaded onto the coach was indeed my job. Yeah! What joy. All I could think about was the excess baggage charge Mr H was about to pay.

It was a huge pain in the arse at the check-in desk, I was surprised they even let us on the plane with all that luggage. God only knows what they had to pay. Of course the Hilton's were in first class again, unlike the trip out though, this time they had booked a cot for Barron. Maybe I'd get a little sleep this time. I was just so ecstatic that we were going back to Los Angeles, I thought nothing could tarnish my delight. My joy was short-lived when I learned that Mrs H had given Barron prunes for breakfast. What intelligent human being would give a small child, prunes for breakfast? Especially just before a long-haul flight. To say there was shit everywhere was an understatement. To add insult to injury the cabin staff told me they only had new born nappies on board. I however had run out just four hours into the flight. Of course I did, Barron had diarrhoea two hours into the flight. Mrs H came by to take Barron for a while, until she saw the state he was in. She went back to first class and that was the last I saw of her until we landed. She left me embarrassed and covered in shit for the entire flight.

Five weeks, five long, long weeks, I had been on vacation with these people. I didn't know how I had survived. I had learnt one thing from this trip, there was not enough money in this world that I would accept to go on another trip with this family. Wendy, Mr H's secretary, was the first smiling face I saw as I came through the gate. She took me to one side and asked if I was okay. I knew I looked really tired, however she later told me that I had left looking like a young girl and returned looking ten years older.

It was down to me and Wendy to get the forty pieces of luggage back to the house. Mimi was the first to greet us, bless her she had missed her little Barron. The maids were eager to take the bags in and I grabbed this wonderful opportunity to go to my room and my bed. I didn't unpack, I just threw myself onto my bed and slept right through to the next day. It seemed forever since I hadn't been woken up by the screams of baba. I was given the next couple of days off. That was big of them.

The next couple of days would be decision time. Did I leave this crazy household, while I still had my sanity. Or stick it out until I had another job and some money behind me. I had a chat with Wendy on the way from the airport, to see if they had any other vacation planned. She assured me that they didn't, it was a yearly event. So I had confirmation that this vacation from hell that I'd just endured, would not be repeated anytime soon. So I would stick it out, at least for the time being.

Getting my Californian driver's licence was a priority right now. The Hiltons wanted me to use their cars, and they were not insured for me. After the episode with the gates at Mr Hilton Senior's house, this was crucial. Plus it didn't hurt to have my licence, in case I did want to apply for other jobs. The test was really easy, nothing compared to the test in England. I took it in the Range Rover which being an automatic car, would not be allowed in England. The examiner chatted to me all the way through the test. I firmly believe that a chimpanzee could pass the California driving test.

The staff had warmed up to me, well ever so slightly. Especially Mimi, who now realised I wasn't trying to take her job or her baba drinking machine from her. I was going to scold Mimi about the bad habits she'd let Barron develop. Then on thinking about it, firstly I wasn't going to have to deal with said habits ever again, and this was a young girl who had no nanny experience, and was too young to have any life experiences. I felt she wasn't to blame. The parents were, so I said nothing.

So here I was three months into the job, and realised my function in the house had never really been explained. The girls were at school, there were maids to clean up and Mimi took care of Barron, so what was my job in this crazy household.

Let me put it this way, I soon became familiar with the layout of some major stores. Neiman Marcus, Saks Fifth Avenue, and I. Magnin to name but a few. Mrs H didn't like to try clothes on in these shops, so she would look, grab her size and leave with armfuls of garments. That way it gave her time to lunch with friends. Once she got home they would be tried on. Either she didn't like them or they didn't fit, so these were returned the next day by moi. One thing that amused me was that the ones that made the cut, were debagged, labels removed, and would hang in her closet in such a way as to appear that they had resided there for a while. I worked out one day that the financial spend was around $1000 a day.

Well if I hadn't worked it out after the trip, I had now. This lady had a serious shopping habit. We had only returned from Europe a week ago with numerous bags of clothes and her she was shopping again. It would be a financial problem for us mere mortals. However for this lady, not a problem per se because Mr H adored his wife, he had the finances to feed her habit, so basically she could buy whatever she wanted. Yeah, I had discovered what one of my jobs entailed. Of course this didn't take all day. Mrs H didn't get up very early in the morning, so I would hang about in the kitchen until she showed her face.

So who was this lady who had married into money? The daughter of Katherine Dugan and Laurence Avanzino. The mother went on to marry Kenneth Richards and they had two daughters, Kyle and Kim, so half sisters to Kathy. They had all been brought up amid the Hollywood lifestyle. Kathy had been an actress, appearing in *Nanny and the Professor, Bewitched, Family Affair, Happy Days* and *The Rockford Files.* She had also been a model. She had met Mr Hilton when she was only fifteen years old, and married him in 1979. Her sisters were also child actresses, with Kim's career being the most successful. She not only worked for Disney for a number of years, but had numerous other movies under her belt. *Meatballs Two, The Car, Tuff Turf,* and her latest movie, *Escape.*

The beautiful Kathy Hilton and me.

The two best known movies being *Escape* and *Return to Witch Mountain,* starring Bette Davis. Their mother obviously wanted the best for her girls and wanted them to not only be successful in their own lives, but also marry rich and successful men. It would never be a difficult task as they were all three very beautiful young ladies.

So Mrs H had married him at just nineteen years old, had Paris one year later on 17th February 1981, Nicky on 5th October 1983, and young Barron on 7th November 1989. It appeared to be a great, happy, family dynamic. Mrs Richards was very proud of her daughter.

Not so proud of her daughter Kim, I expect. Why, you ask? Well Kim had messed up big time. She had managed to snag the son of

Barbara and Marvin Davis, Gregg. This was one of the richest and most influential families in Los Angeles. While she was in the hospital giving birth to their second child, he was at their home packing up his things and moving out. Yes this was not a happy marriage. Her in-laws had set up a high tech security system all round the home, and had hired several security guards to protect their grandchildren. They knew where she was 24/7. So she was unhappy in their marriage. Everyone goes through a rough patch. Still you had to wonder what would make a man leave his wife while she's giving birth to their child.

There was lots of gossip amongst the maids, theories about his departure from the marriage, none confirmed.

She did call the house on day to speak to Mrs H. It was from a drying-out clinic in Chicago. Enough said, this was the wild sister. I loved her before I even met her. She had been married to a really cute guy called Monty, they had a daughter together, Brooke. He came over to the Hilton house one day to pick up Brooke, who was on a play date with the girls. I believed he was far more suited to Kim than stuffy Gregg. He later told a close friend of mine that he still loved Kim, but she had a huge appetite for sex and through the marriage he hadn't been able to satisfy all her needs. So he'd come home one day unexpected and caught her in bed with the gardener. That got me wondering if Gregg had done the same thing. That would explain his departure from the house, maybe one of the many security guards. That amused me.

Kyle Richards, the younger sister of Mrs H, was also married. She had a little girl around Barron's age, and her husband was a prince, apparently. Before I had figured out his nationality, their marriage was also on the rocks.

So here I was in the middle of some really messed-up families. Taking care of some really badly behaved children. Confirming my suspicions that money doesn't always buy happiness.

Another job was revealed at the end of the girl's school holidays. I had to get up at the crack of dawn to make sure the girls were ready for school, and that they were out of the door in time to get on the school bus. Of course they took after their mum, never on time. She'd be late for her own funeral, and her girls were no different.

Mr H had bought me a car for my own personal use on my day off. What a crock of shit. I soon realised that the chance of the girls being ready for the bus in the mornings was zero, so I had been given the car so when the bus left without the little angels, each and every morning, I had to drive them. On what joy.

Me and Barron with my Ford Taurus. A gift with an ulterior motive.

I don't know what it is about rich people, it always seems that the more money they have, the cheaper they are. The Hiltons were no exception. They exploited their staff at every opportunity. Nadi was sweet, she had been living with them for quite some time, she spoke no English and had a son, Antonio. The hours she worked and what she got paid was a joke. The Hilton's reasoning behind this poor pay was that they were not only giving Nadi a home, but also her son.

In the kitchen.
L-R Me, Paris, Nicky, Brooke, Nadi and her son, Antonio.
The birthday cake was for Antonio.

This poor lady had been through hell in her life. One day she showed me the bullet wound in her side, she had received this while crossing the border from Mexico. Mrs H had told me that Nadi and her son were like family. Who exploits their family for cheap labour?

Then there was Mimi, also Hispanic and only a child herself, taking care of little Barron with no nanny experience at all. The heir to a Hilton fortune. It was scary and proved to me just how cheap they really were. The other member of staff was Sarah, she mainly cleaned and tidied up after the girls, she didn't live-in, so could escape at the end of every day. Of course the other members of staff was me, apart from the Hiltons, the only non-Hispanic in the household. I muddled through on a daily basis.

I realised in time that one of my jobs was to bury dead pets. It became clear to me that Paris, nicknamed Star by her dad, only had to pout and fake tears to get whatever she wanted. Just like her mum. Each week came a different fad, one day it might be a cat, or a kitten, dog or puppy. Rabbit, hamster or even rats. Any living thing could die at the hands of Paris. The main cause of death, neglect. The cats usually ran away, they had a better chance of survival dodging traffic on the busy Sunset Boulevard than they had waiting to be fed or taken care of in this household. They were treated alright for the first couple of months. Then the girls would either get bored with them, or the latest fad was introduced into the house.

The $500 cat that ran away after just two months.

Cute little Barron with his cat.

The worst most tragic thing I witnessed was the purchase of two tea-cup poodles. This was back in the day when the breeders of these two tiny little things were more interested in making serious money than for the welfare of these tiny creatures. They were $500 each and Paris had named hers Boucheron, after her mum's favourite perfume.

Me with Boucheron, the teacup poodle who did survive, bless him.

These previous little dogs fitted into the palm of your hands and they came with strict instructions. Not like Mogwai in the *Gremlins* movie. Don't feed after dark! But serious instructions on how and what to feed them. Not to play with them like they were toys. Basic stuff, really. I woke in the night to screams, hysteria and a constant use of the F word. Who was this crazy woman? Had she broken into the house and the H's were trying to escort her off the premises? Actually it was none of the above.

It was Mrs H who was doing all the screaming. Imagine how shocked I was on realising all this foul language was coming from Mrs H's mouth. Apparently one of the puppies had become really sick and she was blaming everyone in the house for the poor thing's condition. While she was ranting I noticed that she wasn't too steady on her feet, a little worse for wear methinks. She then backed up and on stomping her feet on the carpet she managed to come down stiletto heel first on poor Nicky's foot. Leaving a dent in the poor girl's foot. Being in considerable pain she ran to her room and slammed the door. When things had calmed down and we had all agreed that taking the puppy back to the breeders in the morning was the best thing we could do. The H's went to their room and I went in to console poor Nicky as it didn't appear that her mother gave a shit. It was then I realised this poor kid might have been a bit of a brat but she was in need of some serious TLC.

Neither of the girls were responsible enough to adhere to instructions so it was no surprise that one of the little guys had become very sick. We rushed him back to the breeders first thing in the morning. She scolded the Hiltons for not following her instructions, she said she would nurse him back to health and she would let us know when he was alright to pick up. It was almost a week before we received the call to pick the puppy up and I wondered how long it would be before I would need to return him again. I was right he did get sick again and this time when the call came from the breeders, it was to tell us that the puppy had indeed died. To this day I don't know if they told us the truth, or if the breeder just decided the puppy would stand a better chance of survival with another family. The other puppy thrived, much to my surprise. Boucheron was fussed over for a few months, then like all his predecessors he was ignored and neglected.

One day I received a disturbing call from Mrs H's mother. She wanted to speak to her daughter and sounded like a crazy person. I had no idea which restaurant they were dining at and this made her angrier. It wasn't my fault that they cared so little about their family that they didn't even tell me where they were going. I wasn't sure if she was incoherent because she was upset or if she had been drinking. Whatever the case, I couldn't help her. All I could understand was that Kim had been involved, there was a deli in the Valley and someone had been shot. I told her all I could do would be to leave a note on Mrs H's pillow explaining to call her mother, and that it was urgent.

I knew something was wrong. Mrs H was up early in the morning and that never happened, I was summoned to their boudoir and told that the girls were not going to school that day. I was also told that Kim's boyfriend had been shot dead in a deli in the Valley. I wasn't to go anywhere near Kim's house, until I was told it was alright. Nothing more was ever said about the matter. The next thing I knew there was a memorial service being held for him at the Michael Landon Memorial and that Kim was paying for everything. I went round to her home the day of the service and she looked a real mess. It looked like she had been crying every day since this horrible tragedy. I didn't ask any questions and I ignored all the gossip between staff in the house.

Kim was a very attractive young woman and it didn't take her long to find someone new in her life. She advertised the deceased boyfriend's motorbike and the guy that purchased it, started dating her.

I had most weekends off and I tried to get away from the house, so I wouldn't be pestered or persuaded to run some kind of errand for me bosses. However this weekend they were all away. Parents off on a trip, and the children were over at their aunt's home. Yeah, the weather was great so I thought I would sunbathe and take a dip in the pool. It was always covered, I thought this was so they didn't have to get it cleaned all the time. I pulled back the cover and began to enjoy my day free from anyone bugging me. My peace and quiet was short lived. An hysterical crazed woman came running down the lawn, screaming for me to get out of the pool, my god, were there piranhas in the pool. Of course not. Just Mrs H's crazed mother. She was adamant that I should get out of the pool so to shut her up, I did. Still very confused about her behaviour and a little scared of her, I got out the pool.

She told me that the cover was to stay on when the Hilton's were away, for the safety of their children. Once I had explained that the children were not at home and that I was a really good swimmer, she did start to calm down. She still didn't explain all the craziness. However I did get the whole story later. They girls told me that they had a maid who had drowned in the pool. Apparently Paris had been messing around one day and pretended she was drowning. So the girl had jumped in to save her and not being a great swimmer, had drowned herself. Wow, how tragic was that. So this explained why the girls talked about having their own ghost. When they told me about the ghost at Barron's house, they did say that they had their own ghost who roamed the garden.

Young Nicky came to me one day crying, she said she had seen a ghost in the garden. The girls had a tree house and she said things had been moved around. Believing that the ghost lived there, she stopped going up there to play. I told Nicky there was no such thing as ghosts, and I went up to the play house with her. Things had been moved around and I of course had no explanation for her. On several occasions I saw a figure in the garden. The figure appeared to be wearing a maid's outfit. Did ghosts follow this family everywhere? A dead maid and numerous dead pets, it was no wonder that they were haunted by ghosts.

That weekend I got to know Nadi a little better. It's funny, even two people who don't speak the same language can still communicate enough to become friends. This was not an educated woman but was bright enough to know when her bosses were exploiting her. She was of course grateful to them for giving her and her son a roof over their heads. Nadi had a lot of friends who worked in similar homes and were paid a good fair wage, she was paid a pittance. The real shocker was her age, I thought I was misunderstanding her, then Sarah came into the kitchen and I asked her Nadi's age. Really shocked she was actually younger than me, as she looked like a grandmother. I couldn't imagine the life she had had to look that old. She only had one day off a week and she would visit friends. That was when she wasn't taking Antonio to the doctors. He was often sick and having no medical insurance meant she had to pay for all his medical care. Being paid a pittance meant she had no savings, no light at the end of a very dark tunnel. It was no surprise to me that she was always crying, always depressed. Bless her.

A few months later, Sarah told me that Nadi had decided to leave. I would miss her, but on the other hand I was so pleased she'd made a positive decision to improve her life. She didn't want the Hiltons to know she was leaving. I understood that. This was the perfect day. Mr H at work, Mrs H shopping, girls at school. Sarah loaded Nadi's things into her car, that was pretty sad in itself, seeing how few possessions she and Antonio had. Then Sarah drove them over the Nadi's friend's house. I was running errands for Mrs H, so I didn't get to say goodbye.

The girls came home from school and Nicky always ran down to see Antonio. She asked me why their door was locked, and where had they gone. She knew it wasn't Nadi's day off. I of course lied to the poor girl and said I had no idea. I knew that Antonio was like a brother to Nicky, so I did feel sad for her.

Mrs H came back from shopping, arms full of designer bags. I grabbed them to take up to her room. I didn't want to be around when the shit hit the fan, as it inevitably would. Mimi being the sneak and kiss-arse that she was, couldn't wait to tell her Nadi had left, and she tried her hardest to throw us all under the bus, hinting to Mrs H that we all knew about her departure. I didn't lie per se because I said I didn't see Nadi leave and I didn't, because I was out running errands. Mimi made sure poor Sarah got the entire blame. She said that Sarah had not only helped her but had also driven her with all her belongings to her friend's house. Mimi wasn't the sharpest knife in the drawer. One member of staff leaving in a day was enough, but two. These ladies did all the cleaning. Mimi sat on her arse all day, barely taking care of Barron. The reality of her squealing hit her the next day when she was told she would be doing all the cleaning until the two ladies had been replaced. Way to go Mimi, Karma is a bitch.

My birthday was coming up and this year it fell on Labour Day. The H's had made plans to go over the Barron Senior's home for the day. It was a glorious hot, sunny day. So a picnic and a day spent by the pool, not too shabby. I'd not been into this home before, always picking the girls up and staying in the car. It was beautiful inside but not as grand as I'd imagined. This was the home of Papa Hilton, the owner of an entire chain of Hilton Hotels. Little disappointed, thought it would wow me.

The food was all laid out in the pool house and it looked delicious. A glass door was just ajar enough to squeeze through. I went back into the pool house later to change into my swimsuit and when I left, banged my ankle on a large stone statue. A stone statue that hadn't been in the way, when I exited just thirty minutes earlier. I found the girls and asked them if they knew who had moved it. They giggled and I guessed they had something to do with it. They were adamant that they had nothing to do with moving it and they said things moved around this house all the time. I asked them what they meant and they said the ghost that resided there was always moving stuff. Ghosts, ghosts and more bloody ghosts, they were obsessed. However when I went back into the house to get dressed, I felt sure the statue had moved back to it's original spot and I got a chill that ran all the way down my spine. Mrs H came over and asked if I needed anything for my ankle. I told her it was ok, I didn't want to make a fuss, but it was throbbing. She said "Guess the ghost doesn't like you either". I asked her what she meant and she told me she had witnessed all sorts of bizarre things happening in this home and she had taken many a tumble, tripping over things that appeared out of nowhere. "She only does it to people she doesn't like" she said. Had Mrs H got ghost fever too, or had the girls put her up to it.

The maids that worked at Papa Hilton's house had worked there years. They obviously treated their staff better than the son did. One of the maids asked me if I was ok, as I was limping a little. I told her about the moving of the statue, feeling a bit embarrassed as I thought she probably thought me crazy. Then she surprised me by telling me a story about the day she thought the Hilton's had a guest staying that she hadn't been told about. She had been cleaning one of the bedrooms and when she came out of the bathroom, a pretty young woman was brushing her hair in the dresser mirror. She didn't recognise the girl s being one of the grandchildren. So she apologised and rushed out, deciding the lady might want her privacy. She asked another maid who the lady was and was told no one was staying in the room. Yet another shiver ran down my spine. Still I wasn't sure if I was being set up, I'd gotten used to the girls and indeed Mrs H playing pranks on people. Well I had a swollen sore ankle but I had a really nice day. Mrs H had brought me a lovely cake which had been a really nice surprise.

Barron's home was perfect for parties, all the grandchildren had their birthday parties there. Bouncy castles, rides and even petting zoos were just some of the fun things they had for entertainment. I had a friend over from England one day. I took her to one of Nicky's birthday parties, which was being held at Barron's house. Just so she could see that I wasn't exaggerating about the amount of money spent. We are not talking about hundreds, but thousands of dollars.

It took several weeks to replace the maids and Mimi was exhausted doing three people's work. Let's face it, she wasn't used to doing that of one person. Having seen that Mimi could juggle housework and take care of Barron, Mrs H decided that Mimi could do more about the house. A chore rota was set up and I had been given the arduous task of making sure the work was carried out.

So I had been living with family for over six months now. Had I settled in? I guess surviving the vacation from hell in the beginning, had made me a stronger, more resilient person. So had I settled, in, yes, I guess I had.

In those six months I hadn't really encountered anyone famous. That was until the evening of the school recital. There was food and I was starving and loved a buffet. I paid no attention to whom the Hilton's were chatting to, too busy stuffing my face. Lights went down and I grabbed a Seat not far from Mr H. The gentleman next to me said he was a friend of the Hilton's and they had told him I was English. From then on we had a nice chat about how great England was. I had no idea who I speaking to, I hadn't turned towards him and the dimmed lights had made it quite dark.

Then the lights came back on. I turned to say goodbye to this nice gentleman and froze in mid-sentence. I had been chatting for an hour to Lionel Richie, like he was an everyday Joe I just met in a bar. He must have noticed the embarrassed look on my face, hard for me to hide when I go such a wonderful shade of bright red. His daughter Nicole was in the same class as Paris. I wanted to tell him I was a huge fan, that was not going to happen, given that I had been chatting to the man for an hour and hadn't recognised him.

The weekends were my safe haven. I could get away from all the madness. I would drive down to Orange County on a Friday night and stay with a friend, returning on the Sunday. If I stayed in the house, it turned out to be a big mistake. It was always, Diane can you just run the girls here, or Diane just drive there and pick something up for me. Out of sight, out of mind. I made sure I was definitely out of sight. The weekends I didn't go to Orange County, I would stay out all day Saturday, going to a movie or shopping, and return when I knew they had gone out.

This one weekend I could just relax at home, because the Hilton's had gone to Las Vegas and the girls were over at their aunt's house, or so I thought. The Hilton's came home early from their trip. The phone in my room rang and I was very tempted not to answer. Trouble was, my car was in the drive so they knew I was home. It was Mr H, apparently they had just managed to get on their flight, late as usual. Not having time to check-in their luggage, it was coming on the next flight. So he wanted me, on my day off, to drive all the way to the airport to pick it up. Before I had finished cursing to myself, the phone went again. This time it was Mrs H. Paris had rung her and asked to be picked up from a skating rink in Culver City, where she was at a party for Nicole Richie. Apparently she was bored and wanted to come home. I explained that I had no idea where the ice rink was and besides, Mr H had just asked me to drive to the airport to pick up their luggage. I then made a huge mistake, I suggested that Paris get a taxi home.

I hung up the phone, so pissed off with these people, my day off, they wanted me to cut myself in half, and run two errands. What happened next was mind blowing, I heard shouting, slamming of the front door and the screeching of tyres as a car sped out of the drive onto Sunset Boulevard. I wondered what was going on and was soon enlightened. Mr H called to me upstairs, he was shouting at me, how dare I tell his wife that she should get a taxi for their daughter. No Hilton was getting in a taxi. He ranted on that his wife was now in a temper and driving like a crazy person. Hey, you married that crazy person who just drove out of the drive at sixty miles an hour. Well I thought that, I didn't actually say it. I said nothing, I just turned around and walked out. I returned to my room and packed my things. This was the final straw, I couldn't deal with these people any longer. He'd used the 'F' word at me and on one spoke to me like that, especially from this crazy family. I didn't go to the airport to pick up their luggage, I believe they sent a taxi for it.

Of course after sleeping on it, I did wonder if I was making a big mistake leaving. After all, it was coming up to winter time in England. I tested the water by calling Wendy on Monday morning, and said I was giving a week's notice. She said she was shocked and that the H's had said nothing but praise for my work. I told her what happened and how Mr H had cursed me out, using the 'F' word. I told her nothing short of an apology from Mr H was going to keep me there. She said she hadn't heard him apologise, ever, that she felt on more than one occasion, she had deserved one. She told me not to hold my breath, that was never going to happen. I told her then they would be losing me.

That evening a barbecue had been planned, so I helped with the coals and getting it lit. Mr H came over to me and said he didn't want me to leave, and that they were very happy with my work. He didn't actually apologise but he did say that he had spoken out of turn, and that he hoped I would reconsider staying with them. So not an actual apology but I figured I'd take whatever I could get from this man.

I called Wendy in the morning and she was really shocked that I'd received even a half-hearted apology from Mr H. She told me that they must love me because that never happened. So I took back my resignation and lived happily ever after. Come on, this isn't a fairy tale.

One of many birthday parties.
R-L Me, Wendy, Paris and Kathy.

Another weekend off and I was hiding in my room. Yes hiding, I thought if no one saw me they would all think I was out. The Hilton's had gone out for the evening, as per usual, and I just wanted some peace and quiet. Only Mimi remained, taking care of Barron and the girls. My room was in the basement and next door to it there was a gym and games room.

I could hear the girls playing, shouting and running round. As soon as the Hilton's left of an evening, Mimi would be on the phone to her boyfriend or sister, totally oblivious to all that was going on around her. The girls were old enough to take care of themselves, but little Barron should not have been left to fend for himself. I heard a lump, then a scream, then crying. I thought it was Barron and I was getting ready to rip into Mimi, when there was a knock on my door. I was really annoyed now, so much for my peace and quiet, so much for yet another uninterrupted day off. I opened the door expecting to see Barron, but it was Nicky and she already had a lump the size of an egg pulsating on her forehead.

Apparently they had been chasing each other, Nicky had tripped and headbutted a wooden bench. I tried to look calm in front of Nicky because I didn't want to scare her, but shit, I had never seen anyone's forehead swell up like that before. I was really mad now especially with Mimi. I stormed to her room, snatched the phone out of her hand and hung it up. She looked like she was going to snap at me, until she saw the look on my face. I asked her if she knew where the Hilton's were dining that evening and of course she didn't. I grabbed some ice from the freezer, wrapped it in a tea towel and told Nicky to keep it on the bump to help get the swelling down. She said she was tired and wanted to go to sleep.

Ok I have no medical experience but I did know that you shouldn't let a child sleep after a bang on the head, something about going into a coma.

Paris had no idea where her parents were dining, Mimi had no idea, so last resort I called round a few of the restaurants that I knew they frequented. I called a dozen or so and I was getting really anxious about Nicky falling asleep. So I panicked and called the grandmother, not one of my favourite people. She ranted on about the children being our responsibility while the parents were out, and why hadn't we got the number of the restaurant where they were dining. Once I could shut her up, I told her firstly that this was my day off, secondly the parents should leave details of their whereabouts with the staff in case something like this happens. She had no reply and I reminded her of the urgency of the situation. She said she would ring round and find them.

So I carried on walking Nicky round the house, trying to keep her awake. Grandmother called with the phone number of Mr H's car. I called and called for about an hour. Finally he picked up. I told him what had happened and I'm sure he heard the panic in my voice. I could hear Mrs H in the background asking him what the problem was. After he told her she said, we will all be home soon. Mr H said they had somewhere they needed to be and would come straight home after that, not to worry Nicky would be fine. I again emphasised that it was urgent they come home straight away. Of course, they didn't bother to hurry home. Almost an hour had gone by when I heard their car pull up in the drive.

I was near to tears by now and so bloody furious that they hadn't taken me seriously. Mrs H strolled in and went straight to her bedrooms. Mr H did however ask how Nicky was. When I showed him the huge lump on her head, he was shocked. I wanted to say, see I wasn't exaggerating, you stupid man., He rang their doctor and he suggested that Nicky come straight to his surgery in the morning.

I didn't sleep well that night, anger and worry overwhelmed me. When I went to get Nicky up in the morning, I didn't know what to expect. The swelling had gone down slightly, but she had two black eyes. Looked like she had done several rounds with Muhammed Ali.

The Beverly Hills doctor gave me the creeps, there was something about him that wasn't quite right. He seemed more concerned about keeping Nicky out of the public eye, than he did about treating her. He said that Social Services might think she had been involved in some kind of child abuse. What a bloody weirdo. I took Nicky home and she was kept out of the school until the blackness around her eyes disappeared.

The kitchen was the meeting point in the mornings, everyone scrambling to have some breakfast. This morning I had a lovely surprise. Sarah was back to work. Guess the Hilton's realised she was a very valuable member of staff after all. They were going to find out just how valuable she was very soon. Sarah was my rock, I could confide in her about problems I felt existed in the running of the home. You couldn't tell Mimi anything, the little bitch would blab straight to Mrs H. Of course, there was the matter of Mimi getting Sarah fired over the Nadi debacle. Sarah would let her pay for that and this amused me no end.

So, Sarah was back, Nicky was at home nursing two black eyes and I was trying to establish what errands I was running that day. Never easy when Mrs H wouldn't come out of her bedroom or get off the phone long enough for me to speak to her.

After failing to get Mrs H's attention yet again, I started back down the stairs. It was then I heard Sarah shout. Nicky's daily ritual consisted of tormenting her little brother Barron, especially when she was bored. Sarah had enough to do without having to deal with Nicky's nonsense so I hurried over to her bedroom. Sarah was dangling Barron by his feet and patting his back. Then I saw her put her fingers in his mouth and removed what looked like a sweet. Barron's face was bright red, and Sarah had just saved him from choking to death on a hard candy that Nicky had given him. Nicky ran to her room and I was so angry with her.

Sarah was shaking and in tears, I gave her a hug and praised her for being so amazing under all that pressure. I then told her that I wouldn't have a clue what to do and in the hands of his nanny Mimi, his chances of surviving that kind of incident, zero.

So Nicky was hiding in her room, so I went in for a chat. I asked her why she gave Barron a sweet that she knew would choke him. She had been told on many occasions that he was too small for hard candy. I then asked her if she realised that she could have killed him. She said no, and she was really sorry. Those were her words but her face told another story.

So I finally manged to get into Madam's bedroom. I told her about Sarah's heroics, how she had saved Barron's life. Hearing that news you would think a mother would have rushed to the person who saved their child's life, and smother them with hugs and kisses. No words would be enough to show your gratitude. Instead I saw no signs of emotion. Oh she was angry with Nicky for giving him the candy. But Madam just went about her day. This was just like any other day to her. Let's just pretend your son's life was not in jeopardy just hours before.

I went to Nicky's room again to see how she was. She was crying. It was at this moment that I realised this poor girl was just crying out for attention. She hadn't tried to kill her brother. It was her way of saying look at me, I'm here too. Her sister Paris was always going to be the favourite, first born and all that. Daddy had nicknamed her Star, she was always going to get the most attention. So there was Nicky, sandwiched between the first born and the first son. She never really stood a chance. Poor girl felt like she was invisible, I finally realised why she was so unhappy. From that day on I grew very fond of Nicky, she would never be invisible to me.

Mrs H finally surfaced from her room, she was all excited to tell me where they had been the night before. What was more important than getting home to your daughter, who had been injured, basically. Apparently her life was so boring she had decided to buy a store. They were viewing said store last night.

A light had turned on in her head and she realised that getting up at noon, shopping and lunching with friends was not a fulfilling way to spend her life., She wanted a gift store and had found the perfect location. It was at Sunset Plaza. I had heard of it and I knew it was a very expensive shopping area and very prestigious. She explained that she was buying the property as a very nice, established business. It was called The Staircase and had a great reputation amongst all her friends, she had shopped there herself on many occasions. The owners had been there years and had built up said reputation. Now ready to retire, wanted it to go into good hands. My thoughts, big mistake letting them have it. I knew that it would be fun for her, for a while. Then she'd get bored and let it go to ruin. Undoing years of these nice people's work.

They were of course still in talks about the price. She wanted to buy it as an ongoing concern, keeping the name. She also wanted to buy some of the stock and more importantly, wanted the gift-wrapping room including all the wrapping supplies to be part of the deal. This would most definitely cost more than the original asking price.

So this was what they were doing last night when I requested they hurry home because I had concerns for their daughter. This was more important.

Mr H came home from work and I wondered when Mrs H would tell him his son's life had been in jeopardy that day and that Sarah had saved him. Quite an important event you would think. I decided I would tell him, I said nothing about Nicky giving him the candy, she had suffered enough. I just needed to emphasise that Sarah had saved his son's life, that she was indeed a heroine. I know you can't put a price on saving a child's life but a financial reward would have been a nice gesture. She did get rewarded, he said thank you. Here is a woman living on a shoestring, she just saved your son's life and you say thank you. Big deal. Here's a couple of grand, that would be a nice thank you. Did he think we were exaggerating the incident? Or were they just too mean with their money? Maybe Sarah's actions were inconsequential to these self-centred people.

I was shocked by their cavalier attitude to what had happened that day with young Barron. What exactly did parenthood mean to these people. Did they think it ended with the procreation and birth of a child.

Mr H came over to ask me if Mrs H had told me about her new adventure. He was so pleased she had found something positive to do with her life, thinking it would keep her out of Neiman Marcus and all the other Beverly Hills stores she frequented. I wanted to laugh, but looking at his face I saw he was being serious. Poor man, did he really think buying a store for a shopaholic was a wise move. You wouldn't buy a pub for an alcoholic. Same thing, different addiction.

Getting out of the house on my days off would always be the right move. I felt free and happy. Food shopping in Gelson's in Century City one day, I had noticed they had a nice cinema. So that was my goal this day, to see a movie. Multiplex, so lots of choice.

I came from a small city in England, Norwich, so I hadn't met anyone famous in my life, until the night I met Lionel Richie. Even though Los Angeles is overflowing with rich and famous people, I had no idea that on this day I would meet famous person number two. I made my way over to where I thought the ticket queue would be and was really shocked at how long it was. Silly me, I hadn't joined the cinema queue, I'd joined a booking signing line. The book shop was right by the ticket desk, very confusing. As I'd been in the line for quite some time, I thought I'd ask whose book it was. I imagined I'd not recognise the name, not being a great literature buff myself. Dudley Moore was the writer, hey I knew him. One of England's finest comedians. Great pianist and star of the movie *Arthur*. Maybe this wasn't that Dudley Moore, a writer with the same name perhaps. I didn't want to lose my place in the line and sure as hell didn't want to show my ignorance by asking someone in the queue which Dudley it was. So I stayed in the line and thought, if it's not him when I get to the front, I'll just walk away and join the cinema ticket line as planned.

The line moved quite quickly and I could see sitting at the table was indeed lovely Dudley. Yeah, I loved him. The book was entitled *Off Beat*. I purchased a copy and had it ready to be signed by the great man himself. I noticed he was letting people take a photo with him and as luck would have it, I had my camera with me that day. Still a tourist at heart. When I got up to him, I couldn't help but notice how tired he looked. It wasn't surprising, that was one hell of a queue of people, I didn't know he was so popular in America.

He had his "people" standing beside him and I politely asked one of them to take my photo with Dudley, he obliged and took two just to be sure.

Book signing, me and Dudley Moore.

Attempting to speak to famous people when you are a little shy and star struck isn't easy. However I didn't want a repeat performance of the Lionel Richie debacle. I opened the book and he signed it *To Diane from Dudley Moore,* as expected. Then he realised my accent was English, and he asked me what part of England I was from. When I said Norwich he began to smile and said he had visited there lots of times and loved it. He had been on the Norfolk Broads too and said that part of England was beautiful. He then asked me if I was on holiday and not wanting to get into the whole living with the Hilton's thing, I said I was. He then asked for the book back and I wondered what he was doing, I could see he was adding something to his autograph. As soon as I got out of the shop, I opened the book to see what he had added. In brackets he had added *love!* I wanted to thank him, but going back to speak to him would take a lot more courage than I had. I had a silly smile on my face for the rest of the day. I can't even tell you what movie I saw that day. I would go on to meet many famous people in the time I spent living in Los Angeles, but none will be as memorable, or treasured as much as meeting Dudley Moore.

He called me back to add Love to his signature.

What an amazing man. I saw him again a few years later. He co-owned a restaurant in Venice Beach, called 72 Market Street Oyster Bar & Grill. He was playing piano. I glanced over a few times and he smiled. I was sure he wouldn't remember me from our brief meet years earlier. When he'd finished, he headed for my table and said "Miss Norfolk, right?". I went a little red and told him I was surprised he remembered me. He just smiled back and left the restaurant. I thought he didn't look that well. Rumours then went round that he was the subject of domestic abuse. Not little pint size 5'2" Dudley, no he wasn't the abuser, the 4th wife was abusing him, beating him up any chance she got, and all I wanted to do was cuddle him.

Negotiations for the store went on for a few weeks. Once they were complete Mrs H spent most of her time there, organising decorators, hiring staff and the most important thing, buying stock. She had found someone to manage the store and for some reason wanted me to come along and meet her. She seemed like a lovely lady and I wondered if she knew just what was in store for her. The rest of the staff seemed nice too, which was great. By now I realised I'd be spending quite a lot of time at the store, helping out with things. The store was spacious now, less cluttered than it had been with the previous owners. I had to hand it to her, it did look great.

Over the next few weeks I spent a lot of time there helping the staff get it ready for the big opening. Mrs H had hired a professional Christmas decorator, hey who knew there was such a thing. Only in L.A. The way this guy decorated trees blew my mind. Of course, a fully decorated tree costs not hundreds but thousands of dollars. However, the clientele that frequented the Plaza had that kind of money.

Opening party at the Staircase. That's me behind
the counter surrounded by Christmas.

An opening night party, with celebrity guests was a great idea, on paper. All the guests have to turn up on the night though, and the majority of them were no shows. Sylvester Stallone did turn up and it was soon obvious he'd come for the free food and drink. I think he'd already been to a few bars before arriving at the party. It had been a huge expense, the marquee erected in the car park, staff and food had run into thousands, but the comments about the amazing decorated trees and the gifts on sale were all very positive. Everyone appeared to be having a great time, in spite of several no-shows. So the aim of the party was to let everyone know Mrs H now owned the Staircase and to showcase the stock and the amazing trees. Hey, job done.

We opened in the October. The store looked like Santa's grotto. An amazing version of it anyway. Selling the trees fully decorated was the main aim. Some people would just take the ornaments hoping to copy Bob's look in their own homes. Others would pay for the whole package, this would include the tree, ornaments and him coming to your home to dress it. This was a huge success. It's amazing how many people in L.A. have too much money and are too lazy to decorate their own trees. That's half the fun as far as I'm concerned.

A wonderland of gifts and Christmas decorations.

Celebrities came through the door on a daily basis. Bruce Springsteen and wife, Priscilla Presley, Ringo Starr, to name just a few. Everyday was a game of name the celebrity. So everything looked fabulous and for the first time since I joined the Hilton family, I was actually quite happy.

Mrs H had great taste and the gifts she bought for the store ran off the shelves. It seemed everyone was into cherubs, angels and anything that had been decoupaged. Scented candles and pot-pourri from all over the world kept the store alive with copious fragrances.

I spent more and more time at the store and less at the house. I really liked these changes to my working life.

Christmas Day came and it seemed strange not being in England with my own family. Strange and horrifying was watching the children unwrap their Christmas gifts. They were piled to the ceiling. I watched them for about fifteen minutes. These ungrateful monsters ripped off the gift wrap acting like it was a chore. Many of the gifts had been sent over from Barron's house. There were dresses that had been purchased from top Beverly Hills stores and had cost hundreds of dollars. These were the first to be thrown across the room in disgust. Then Nicky had received a gift that Paris had wanted and war broke out. Watching them fight over this one gift was sickening and disgraceful. I'd had enough. Mrs H had mentioned earlier she still had a couple of gifts to wrap that she needed to take over the Barron's home that evening. I quickly volunteered to go to the store and wrap them for her, anything to get out of this mad house. I stayed at the Plaza for quite some time enjoying the peace and quiet. When I arrived back at the house it was time for lunch. The only part that resembled a traditional English Christmas dinner was the turkey. The rest was awful. I guess it was hardly surprising, the whole dinner was cooked by two maids who only really knew how to cook burritos and tacos.

Thinking it couldn't get any worse was a big mistake. The Hilton's invited me to Barron's house for the evening. I hadn't realised this family was so big, I thought Mr H was an only child. That really wasn't the case. He was one of eight children. Five brothers and two sisters. Brothers Steven, Daniel, William, Ronald and David. Sisters Sharon and Hawley. Eight children plus their partners made quite a gathering.

These were not warm and friendly people. In fact I felt about as welcome as a dose of diarrhoea. Mr and Mrs H didn't really treat me like that, I never felt beneath them, that was one thing I did appreciate about them. Barron however looked at me like I was something he'd scraped off the bottom of his shoes. Needless to say, I was really glad when that little shindig was over.

Christmas was finally over and now we needed to prepare the store for a sale of all Christmas related goods, I hadn't realised just how much Christmas stock we had until we started to sort it out.

I had to go to the office to see Wendy and pick up the staff wages. She told me that the Hilton's went to Las Vegas every year for New Year and they had asked her to invite me as their guest. New Year fell on a weekend so I wouldn't be working. If course I was apprehensive about going. Past experiences had taught me one thing, when they said free time, it didn't mean I wouldn't get stuck with looking after the children. Wendy then assured me that I wouldn't, and that I would have a great time. I had never been to Vegas so what the hell, it did sound like fun.

Big mistake, you'd think I would have learned a lesson from the European trip. Hey, a mug and pushover springs to mind. Not only did I get landed with looking after the Hilton girls but their friends too. I did have one bit of fun. Barron looked really cute, he was dressed in a tuxedo and top hat. Mimi was nowhere to be seen and he had decided to dance on the main dance floor. As I watched him security came running over to remove him. I enjoyed telling these guys that this little boy was the owner's grandson and I felt if he wanted to dance there, he probably would be allowed to. They apologised profusely, and scurried away.

Me and Barron in hotel at Las Vegas, New Year's Eve.

I tracked down the girls, they were playing in the children's area and Nicky was complaining that one of the machines had taken her money and not given her a go. She had already complained to the guy in the kiosk and he had done nothing about it. I went over and after explaining who Nicky was and telling him how upset she was, he came straight over and put lots of credits into the machine for her. I smiled, I liked this new power I had. So I didn't see the New Year in how I would have liked, but being in Las Vegas, even with this family, wasn't all bad.

So we just made the plane home, no surprise there. Nicky was messing around on the moving walkway and as she slid off, banged her knee. Of course she shouldn't have been messing around, but I knew she had hurt her knee quite badly. It was obvious she was in pain. Nicky wasn't a baby, she was now eight years old, and didn't cry for no reason. Mrs H was not going to stop and help her daughter, so I did. She could barely walk and I seemed to be the only one who gave a shit. She cried the whole flight and I suggested she be taken to the hospital on our arrival in Los Angeles. The H's disagreed and said they'd make an appointment for her to see the doctor in the morning. Great, was this the doctor I'd met when Nicky had a black eye. Creepy or what?

Mrs H was far too eager to get to her store In the morning. She couldn't take time out for her daughter, so I took her. She hadn't had any sleep and couldn't put weight on the leg at all. After a couple of x-rays it was determined that she had torn a ligament in the knee. They strapped it up for her, gave her crutches and told me to make sure she kept off it for at least a week. Poor Nicky had trouble getting in and out of bed, and the maids weren't always around to help her. So this one occasion she wet the bed. She was so embarrassed. So that it wouldn't happen again I put a nappy on her before I left the house. I had grown very fond of Nicky and felt so sorry for her, she was clearly neglected by her mum. She finished up being off school for almost a month.

Neither of these girls could afford to be away from education for too long. I remember Paris asking me one day if I had learnt American before I had moved there. At first I wondered what she meant, maybe my accent? Then horror, I realised she thought I came from a country that didn't speak English. I told her I came from England, and she asked if they speak American there. How did I explain this to someone who had no clue? So I told her that Americans spoke English with a different accent. I wanted to go into the whole England existed before America thing, but hey, for me to give an entire history lesson to someone that looked like the lights were on but no one was home, was a complete waste of my time.

Another time I was asked if Jesus got two lots of presents, as he was born on Christmas Day. Religious studies were obviously not practised at their school. Like I said, crucial these girls attended school at all times. Not a good idea for them to miss any of their education.

One of my many duties in the household was to grocery shop. I would go to Century City and shop at Gelson's. A nice store and quite expensive, so I stood the chance of seeing someone famous in there. Which I did from time to time. On this one occasion it was pouring down with rain and a man who begged for money outside each and every day was getting soaked. I didn't usually give in to beggars, but this one time seeing him shivering and soaking wet, tugged at my heart strings, so I did.

On my return to the house, I unloaded the groceries and told Mrs H about the poor soaked man and how for once I had given him some money. Her reply to me "I think God sends the rain to wash all the bums away". Mind blowing, these words from a self-professed benevolent and charitable woman.

She wasn't emotionally charitable to her family either. Her sister Kim had been through a lot of pain and heartache. This was the sister I liked and had a lot of empathy for. She had just had surgery for an ongoing problem in her womb and Mrs H called me at the store to go and fetch flowers from her favourite florists, the Empty Vase. I took them straight back to the house. When I arrived there Mrs H was already on her way out the door. She quickly told me the words she wanted written in her sister's card and told me to deliver them. She couldn't take five minutes out of her life to visit her sick sister. I went to Kim's home and the maid led me up to her bedroom. I felt nervous, did she think her sister would be coming through the door? I guess she wasn't expecting to see Mrs H, because the broadest smile came on her face when I entered the room. She looked so sick and it made me very teary eyed. My tears were not only for her appearance but for the fact she was so pleased to see someone, even a near stranger. Imagine how pleased she would have been if her sister had bothered to bring the flowers and write in the bloody card herself. I stayed a while, she looked like she needed the company. She even showed me the scars on her tummy from the keyhole surgery. I didn't know what fibroids were, but it was clear they were very painful.

The children were back at school and making sure they caught the bus on time was my main objective. This meant my working hours were getting longer and longer, I was helping in the store getting the sale ready and constantly getting phone calls from Mrs H, needing me to go here, there and everywhere running errands. I don't believe any of the gifts that came from Barron's home were appreciated. Mrs H saw these gifts as a means to an end. Chicanery being her middle name, she had me return 90% of them, even the children's. Returned and credited to her credit card. These were a lot of gifts and it took me several days.

I had developed a bad cough, which kept me up at night, to the point of being sick. I thought this was probably due to exhaustion and sleeping in a damp room. There was a pathway running beside my room and the rain would run down the outside wall. Yes, California doesn't have a lot of rain but the little it had seemed to penetrate my bedroom wall. There was a musty smell in my room and to me the carpet was a little damp. I told Mr H about my concerns and he said he would have it looked at. I don't believe he ever did. When I told Wendy on the office, she said the house, which had been up for sale for quite some time, now had a buyer. I wasn't even aware it was up for sale.

So of course, they were not going to spend any money on it now. Why pay money out for a damp course to be put in when some mug had already put in an offer for it. How long would the purchase take to be completed? Was I happy with this life, a life that consisted of twelve-hour working days and a very unhealthy cough? Had I come to the end of my adventure? I began to ask myself all of these questions. I wasn't sure I wanted to play in this world anymore, a world of money, and greed. A world where having money meant you were more important than an everyday Joe. Was this reality or had I been absorbed into a movie in La La Land.

It was Mrs H's birthday and Wendy had been given the task of arranging the delivery of the gift to the house. I looked out of the window and there sitting on the drive, was a Rolls Royce Bentley decorated with a huge red bow.

Kathy's birthday present from her husband.
Just a Rolls Royce Bentley!! With a red bow.

A party at Chasen's, the once famous restaurant, was arranged for the evening bash. Wendy and myself were both invited, to look after the girls, I'm sure. Paris always being the one who needed to be the centre of attention, decided she would dance on the tables. No expense was spared, the food was delicious and all in all, I did have a lovely time.

Trader Vic's, Hilton Hotel.
Mr Hilton's birthday party. Paris always had to be the centre of attention. Dancing on tables her speciality.

For a brief time, I was lulled into a false sense of happiness. I'd have a great day up at the Plaza in the store. I loved my new found friends there, we had so much fun when Mrs H wasn't there. Now the novelty had worn off having her on shop. She only visited when she wanted to buy stock. So constantly meeting famous people in the store, enjoying great weather and saying goodbye to these great new friends wasn't going to be easy. However I had made up my mind. I had given it a year. The bad days, working too many hours and my very unhealthy cough, had made my decision a little easier.

The H's were going to New York for a long weekend and the girls were staying at their aunt's house, so this was the perfect time for my escape. I left them a nice letter at the store with Connie. I told them my mother was unwell and that I had returned to England. This was not a complete lie, my mother hadn't been well for quite some time and I had been concerned about her, and of course missed her. I drove to the store, leaving the car and keys there. So Bob "Mr Christmas" took me to the airport. Goodbye L.A., I will miss you.

So here I was back in sunny England. It was only March so they were still having cold and wet weather and would be for a few more months. It didn't take long before I began wondering why the hell I'd come back home. There was a big part of me that wished I'd stayed in Los Angeles. I missed the store, the friends I had there and I missed the every day excitement of meeting celebrities. The buzz up at the Plaza, the overflowing restaurants full of rich and wannabe famous people. Norwich seemed like such a dull place by comparison. And what I missed most of all was the Californian sun.

The summer arrived and with it a smile on what had been a very sad face. I managed to snag a great job as receptionist at a great hairdresser, and I'd decorated my home really nice. Life seemed much brighter now. Was I still pining for my previous life, I'd be lying if I said no. But focusing on the down side of living there, the H's, the naughty children, long working hours, damp room, made me snap back to reality and appreciating my life back at home. My thoughts of naughty children didn't include Nicky. I did miss her, I had become very fond of her and I knew she would be very sad about me leaving, bereft at the prospect of not having me around. I didn't even say goodbye to her.

Just as I'd convinced myself that life in England wasn't so bad, I blinked and the summer was over. Now I was faced with the prospect of cold, wet, windy and probably snowy days. Felicitations Diane, did you make the biggest mistake of your life?

Fate has a funny way of kicking you in the arse on occasions. I'd had a lot of pain in my stomach and deciding it was probably just indigestion, I'd spent the day taking Gaviscon tablets. Once the pain had become debilitating and I was rolling around on the floor, I called the doctor. He took one look at me and called an ambulance. I had a burst appendix and it took me a while to heal from the ordeal. Good old NHS. I tried to imagine what kind of bill I would have received in America for the same treatment. It would have run into thousands, because I had no medical insurance in the time I lived there. Someone was looking out for me, making sure I was in England when this catastrophe struck. Once I was back on my feet, I found out that my job had expired. They had run the reception fine without me so they no longer needed my services. Hey, shit happens.

My friend Shelley was home visiting her family for Christmas. She was the friend I had spent some weekends with in Orange County, when I needed time away from the Hilton house. She had a dual passport, because she was born in America. Her father lived and worked there when she was born. So she went backwards and forwards all the time. Having seen the life I had in Beverly Hills she had decided to go back and instead of living in Orange County with her godparents, had chosen to live and work in Los Angeles. She had rented an apartment with a friend and managed to get a great job in a nice boutique. What she hadn't realised was that I had returned to Norwich.

Her parents told her I'd tried to get in touch, so we arranged to meet for coffee. I knew she would try and persuade me to go back. Hey, it was never going to be a huge task. Let me see, I had no job and a strong aversion to British winters. She told me I could stay in their apartment until I got myself sorted out with a job. So as soon as Christmas and New Year were over, I advertised for someone to rent my flat from me and made my plans to return to Los Angeles.

Their apartment was very spacious and although I was sleeping on a couch, it was very comfortable. I didn't think it would be for long anyway. Once I settled and got over the jet lag and time difference, I called my dear friend Connie at the store. She seemed really pleased to hear from me and even more delighted to know I wasn't just on vacation but had returned, at least for a while. She then whispered to me that Mrs H was in the store and did I want to speak to her? Connie said that Mrs H only said really nice things about me and had no animosity towards me. That was a real surprise. After hearing this from Connie, I figured it wouldn't do any harm. When she came on the phone she was so nice to me, I actually felt a pang of guilt.

She said they had all missed me, especially Nicky, and straight off the bat asked me if and when I was coming back to work. She went on to explain that they had moved and that they had a beautiful house in Bel Air, and it had a guest cottage which would be mine. Before I thought about what I was saying I told her yes. My friend was not only surprised when I told her I not only had a job, but a place to live too. She did remind me about a previous conversation I'd had with her, regarding how arduous my life had been, working for those people. She said there was no hurry for me to find a job or move out. Had I been too impetuous? I slept on it and in the morning, I realised that I might not get a better offer. I hadn't a Green Card and I didn't want to go back to changing nappies on obese children down in the Valley. Hell, I'd come quite a long way since then, it would be silly to waste such as opportunity.

My friend gave me and my belongings a lift to the store. Mrs H arrived shortly after so I didn't have much of a chance to chat to Connie, or to have a well needed catch up, on her life or mine. However she did manage to tell me what the new house was like. Mrs H had wanted her opinion on the décor, as Connie was a designer, she had taken her along on their first viewing of the property. Connie told me it was beautiful and that the previous owner, Jaclyn Smith, had kept it immaculately.

As we pulled into the drive my first impression was that it looked like a beautiful English home. Not what I was expecting at all. I was shown to my new home, the "guest cottage", by none other than Mimi. She actually seemed pleased to see me too. So this cottage was for guests. It was more like a play house for the girls, but I wasn't going to be put off. I was away from the house, I had a modicum of privacy and it didn't appear to be damp. So what the hell.

I went into the house in the morning, wanting to see my Nicky more than anyone else. I had a really frosty welcome from her and although it was upsetting for me, I did kind of understand why she reacted that way. I just hoped one day she would forgive me for leaving the way I did. Mr H was leaving for the office and he smiled, not a natural expression for this man. He gave me some keys and told me they had kept my car and that it was still insured for me to drive. So in one day I'd got myself a job, a place to stay and a car, not too shabby methinks.

Back to L.A. after being home in England. Outside new home in Bel Air.
L-R Me, Paris, Barron and maid Sarah.

I couldn't wait to get to the store. I gave Connie a great big hug and realised there was a whole lot less of her to hug. I had thought the day before, that she'd lost some weight. This was now confirmed. She was never a big lady, but now there was nothing on her. I asked her how she'd managed to lose so much weight and she said it was a very sore subject. Apparently while I was in England, Connie had been taking these really expensive slimming tablets, $200 a month. These were supplied to her by Mrs H. She was getting fed up spending so much money every month just to stay slim, so was seeking an alternative. These suppliers knew that they had these ladies by the short and curlies because there was no other pills on the market that worked as well. Connie knew Mrs H was friends with Mark Hughes, "Mr Herbalife", and he had to have a chemist on hand. She spoke to Mrs H about meeting with Mark, speaking to him about using his chemist to break down the ingredients in the pills. Then maybe he could manufacture them at a lower price.

Connie envisaged a nice financial reward from Mark, after all she was giving him an idea that was sure to be very lucrative.

However, Connie had made a big mistake. Mrs H had seen serious dollar signs and behind Connie's back, arranged a meeting with Mark, with every intention of cutting Connie out. She went to him with "her" great idea to manufacture these pills. So one lawyer and some signed papers later, the H's had themselves a very nice financial Herbalife. They received a very nice cheque each month, their percentage from sales as per their agreement, Connie of course never saw a dime. The only plus had been that she no longer paid $200 for the pills, she now bought the Herbalife formula.

There had been a couple of staff changes in the store while I was away. Thankfully my friend Bob was still there. He was my confidante, we often chatted about my problem of not having a Green Card. A new face was Bob's friend, Dallas. I knew he had to be gay, all Bob's friends were. He had come to visit from Scottsdale, and had been put to work in the store, helping Bob pack up all the Christmas decorations. A nice guy, and I soon realised that Bob had told him about my dilemma. After chatting to him for quite some time he hinted that for a small fee, he could make that possible by marrying me. When I told Connie she thought it was a good idea. Bob not so keen, I think he was secretly in love with Dallas and didn't want to share him.

Outside the Store.
L-R Bob "Dr Christmas", Connie, Bob's friend Dallas, and me.

As the days went by and I chatted some more with him, I did begin to warm to the idea, he was a nice good-looking guy and it wasn't as if he expected me to have an intimate relationship with him. Or was he? I decided to discuss with Dallas what exactly he was expecting from the marriage, other than a financial reward.

Shock! Horror! He told me he wanted children. After I picked myself up off the floor, I told him I thought he was gay and I'd thought it was going to be a marriage of convenience. Apparently this guy was bisexual and wanted a real relationship with me, who knew. Well not for me, that's for sure. Good looking or not I had no intentions of marrying this guy for real. Even fewer intentions of having children with him.

Shortly after my rejection he returned to Dallas, married his childhood sweetheart and went on to have two children with her. Bob never stood a chance, did he.

My next proposal came in the form of T.J., another friend of Bob's, this time really gay. Such a shame, because he was gorgeous. In that part of town usually the gorgeous ones were. He worked for a company that sold personal alarms, not unlike mace or pepper sprays. However, this alarm was electric, no not a stun gun, they were highly illegal. It was a machine with a button that you pressed when you felt you were in danger, it set off such a loud noise anyone attempting to attack you would leg it immediately. This was a two-in-one alarm, in that you could set it up in your home to protect you from intruders. This was not just sales, this was a pyramid scheme and everyone knows that the only people getting rich working on one are the guys at the top. Anyway, he did persuade us to have a go and we all made some money from it. Nowhere near the figure he suggested but hey ho, we gave it a try.

Getting back to my second proposal. T.J. had heard, I'm sure through Bob, that I wanted to marry to get my Green Card. So he offered his own services for a fee of $3000. Forgetting of course that he was gay and only doing it for the money. So how was I going to live with this gorgeous, cute guy in a platonic relationship? This would be an impossible scenario of course. So I told him no go. I later found out that he didn't know we would have to live together to prove to the authorities that we were a couple, so it would have been a no from him anyway, so just as well. My third proposal would come later, now that's a story worth telling.

The new house was a little dark, and had a cold chilling feel to it. The design was European, a mixture of French Estate and English cottage. It was the ivy growing all over the building that gave it the English cottage feel. It was a lot bigger than their previous home. I was not however very impressed with it. I told Connie how I felt and she said when she had viewed it with the Hilton's she had thought it beautiful. It had been featured in the Ideal Homes magazine. I knew Connie had been an interior designer before working for the H's, so I valued her opinion as did they. So what did Connie see that had gone right over my head. She had the magazine out back and showed me how it had been showcased. I stared at the photos in total disbelief, how was this the same home? I said, "It's amazing what these magazines can do with a little airbrushing". Connie insisted that the photos showed the home exactly how she had viewed it with the H's. I told her it looked nothing like that now and I felt she wouldn't recognise it.

It was a few weeks later that the H's went out of town, spending the weekend at Palm Springs. I took that opportunity to get Connie to come over and view the damage done to this beautiful home. A home that she had loved. Looking back, probably not one of my best ideas. I opened the door to a very teary lady, she was upset by the damage done to the outside, so showing her the assault on the inside was not going to cheer her up any. Her tears were not just about the décor, it was about the destruction of paint on doors, doors that were now hanging off their hinges. Paintwork scuffed, carpets and upholstery dirtied. She was amazed how a family could destroy such beauty in such a short amount of time. Locusts sprung to mind.

Life was now a little easier, having my own separate space away from the house. However things were still hard. The hours I worked were too long and the job didn't end with the closure of the store at six. Mrs H would ring me and ask me to pick up something on the way home, either from a store or to pick up takeaway for the girls. Silly me, this was why they gave me back my car, always an ulterior motive with these people.

Then came the night I had been conned into babysitting the children from hell. I say conned, probably duped would be a better terminology. The H's had these friends, I say friends lightly. I never quite believed or understood this friendship. The woman looked like a hooker and her husband was sleazy looking and had an obvious drinking problem. Now enters their offspring. Three boys, each a year apart in age.

Mr H was sitting in the kitchen with me when the monsters tore in, demanding Mrs H get them something to eat. The eldest looked at me and he had the blackest scariest eyes I had ever seen. Mr H and I looked at each other and laughed, it wasn't easy to amuse Mr H. He always had a very serious persona, but on this occasion we both joked about looking for sixes on the boy's head. I then noticed that one of the children had a missing finger, and I joked that his brother had probably chopped it off. I shivered when Mr H told me that's exactly what had happened.

It was a Friday evening and the girls were over at their aunt's house having a sleepover with their cousins. So there was just Mimi and myself. Normally I would just leave Mimi to get on with taking care of Barron. But at Mr H's behest I said I would watch out, in case these boys get a little too boisterous with him. I did feel that his life probably depended on me looking out for him.

These were not normal children, they were, I'm sure, the devils spawn. Apart from wrecking everything they laid their grubby little hands on, I feared for Barron's life the whole time they were there. I just caught one of them pulling over a bookcase that would have fallen on his head. I told Mimi to get him to bed, it was early but like me she realised he probably wouldn't survive another onslaught from these kids. So what had only been three hours had seemed like the longest three hours of my life. The doorbell rang and there stood the parents. The woman who had given birth to the monsters and the man who had impregnated her. Hallelujah, now take them out of my sight.

So where were the H's? Why had these two come to the house alone? He was blind drink and kept making passes at me. She tried to round up her kids, with little or no success. The phone went and it was Mr H, he was asking me if they had gone yet. I explained that they were waiting for them to arrive home and that the man was blind drunk and making passes at me. He said they didn't want to see them and that I should tell them they had gone somewhere urgently and wouldn't be coming home anytime soon. That they said their goodbyes and would ring them soon.

I thought they would leave nice and promptly after hearing that, but they still left in their own sweet time. I would have been concerned about a man driving his children in that state of blind drunkenness. Given it was this obnoxious man and these children, sorry but I had no concern whatsoever. Well maybe a little concerned for whoever was on the roads that night. The H's called again to check that the coast was clear and they could come home. They told me what an awful evening they had and that he had been drunk the whole time. I interrupted their story with one of my own to tell. How the naughtiest, scariest children had wrecked their home, almost killed young Barron and aged me by ten years. I told them under no circumstances was I ever going to watch over those monsters again and not to get me started on the drunken lech they called dad. They of course laughed. Amazing what this pair found amusing.

When I was back home in England, I realised I hadn't done any touristy things in my first stay here, a missed opportunity. So I wasn't going to make the same mistake this time around. On my weekends off I visited every place I could. Mostly on my own, but if my friend Shelley was around I went with her. I started with Hollywood, the place where Richard Gere met Julia Roberts. In the movie it looked like a seedy place and sure enough it looked pretty seedy in daylight too.

So, first impressions not good. I went to the Chinese Theatre and walked along the Hollywood Walk of Fame. There were too many shops selling very tacky crap, and too many people dressed in tacky lookalike costumes. The handprints of some very famous actors and musicians were cool, I guess that made the journey up there worthwhile. However, feeling there was a possibility I could get mugged in broad daylight was a little nerve wracking, to say the least.

When I was working at the store one day, I had a call from Mrs H asking if I could go down town and pick up some frames, from one of our suppliers. She had promised one of her friends that not only would they be in that day, but that they would be gift wrapped and ready for her to pick up that evening. Of course, Mrs H had forgotten to order them. My first thoughts, why me. I knew it was going to be one hell of a drive and in an area I wasn't familiar with. Mrs H said she had written down the directions for me, and they were very simple. Now this was before the time of mobile phones and SatNav, so getting lost was always going to be problematic.

Now let me break this down for you. There were good parts of down town and bad parts of down town. The good parts were straight down Wiltshire Boulevard. There was the financial district. The Staples Centre, you would go there to watch the Lakers play basketball. The Convention Centre, then some market shops, where if you knew the right people, you could pick up a copy designer handbag. Good district. The metro train station and the high-rise offices owned by lawyer firms and banks, etc.

The bad part was where the L.A. riots stemmed from, April 29th 1992. I'd just gone home and the riots began when a policeman had been acquitted of the murder of Rodney King. There were 12,111 arrests, 567 killed and 700 injured. They ransacked shops, and rioted all the way up to Beverly Hills.

So, armed with my directions, I head out to pick up these silver frames. The freeway was going to be the quickest way to get there and I hated driving on them. A sign would suddenly tell you to exit and if you were not in that nearest lane, you had no time at all to get across. I was pleased with the instructions, they were at least quite clear. I exited easily and felt quite assured that I'd driven as directed. However, the buildings started to look a little shabby and it got worse, some were boarded up. My heart was beating quite fast now and I recalled it only beating that fast once before. It was when I was in Greece, the mainland, a place called Kitzi Vari. I was supposed to be a nanny to this little girl, Thamese, and we went for a walk one day, down this dusty road. I saw what I thought was a litter of cute puppies, they were thin and crying. I rushed back to the house to get them milk and some food for mum, who I hoped was around somewhere. She was around alright, and when she appeared out of the bushes, it was pretty apparent that she had rabies. I dropped the dishes of food and held Thamese's hand really tight while we slowly backed up.

I could hear my heart beating in my chest and when I felt we had backed up far enough away from this barking, frothing-at-the-mouth dog, we legged it up the road, as fast as our legs could carry us.

So here I was in another Kitzi Vari situation. This time it wouldn't be a rabid dog, but possibly a coloured person with a hatred for white people, and he could be wielding a gun. I knew if I carried on driving, chances were I'd end up in the middle of this maze of derelict buildings. So I took a chance, and pulled over to ask directions from to women they looked like they might help me. As they looked into the car and saw this white girl, they were shocked. This is all the woman said, and all she needed to say to get me moving. "You lost girl? You better get your white ass out of here, turn around, take the next right and get back on the freeway. You need to do that as fast as your white ass allows".

This white ass nearly soiled itself, but got the heck out. I drove on the freeway for two hours before I realised I was heading in the wrong direction, so once I got off and back on going towards Beverly Hills. I arrived back at the store eight hours after I had left and without those bloody frames.

Driving up to the house one day I noticed a flyer pinned to a post. At first I thought I had read it wrong, so I parked up and went back to check what it said. The flyer had been printed by someone looking for Jaclyn Smith, and they were offering a reward of $2000. I ripped it off the post, folded it up and put it in my pocket.

I knew the exact address of Jaclyn, she still had the odd piece of mail that went to the house, so I would collect it up and every few weeks take it over to her new home. I had a dilemma, on one hand it would be nice to get $2000 for just giving someone information. On the other, would I feel a pang of guilt about giving a potential stalker her address. I kept the flyer in my pocket for a few days while I contemplated the situation.

If this person was close to Ms Smith, he would have known her new address, after all she had only moved down the street. I decided to tell Connie, mainly to get a second opinion. She felt that if someone was crazy enough to pay me $2000 for the address, then I should do it. I called him to find out what his story was. He told me that he was an old friend of Ms Jaclyn and that he had done lots of odd jobs for her at Stradella, now the H's residence. He had been away for a while, and when he went round the house to see her, the new owners said she no longer lived there, and wouldn't give him her new address.

I don't know if I was being naïve but I did give credence to his story. I arranged to meet him at the store and told him I would take him to the house. Connie had arranged for her husband to come with me in anticipation of this guy being a psycho. He looked like Joe Normal in person, so I took him to the house and he gave me a cheque for the $2000, which of course I deposited immediately. No surprise later when I found out he'd put a stop on said cheque. Hey, I was never a very good judge of character.

The surprises kept coming. I received a call from the same man apologising for ripping me off. He said after I dropped him off, he thought I had cheated him and taken him to the wrong address. Then he received a call from a man telling him he knew where she lived. It turned out to be the same address so he gave the guy $1000 and was it ok for him to just pay me the $1000. Hey, I was amazed to get anything out of it. I banked the cheque he brought me in and this time it cleared.

I knew the H's still owned their house on Sunset, it had fallen in and out of escrow several times. Hardly surprising given it had numerous damp problems, a resident ghost and had a pet cemetery for the numerous dead animals previously owned by the girls. So there was finally a sale agreed, and a completion date. I was summoned over there to help Mrs H sort through their belongings. I was shocked to see that the house looked the same as I had left it over a year ago. It looked like they had just moved and left everything in this life behind. Sad and somewhat eerie. I couldn't imagine why none of these items had any meaning to owners, they were mere objects tossed aside. Seeing all the furniture, kitchen utensils, pots and pans, crockery and personal items, I realised that everything in the new house had been bought, nothing was taken from this home. An example of what people with too much money can achieve.

Mimi was already there and after seeing this mound of belongings in Mrs H's room, I was relieved I'd have some help. We opened Mrs H's closet and there laid all her make-up, shoes, handbags, jewellery and a rail of her clothes. Shit, had she taken anything of her personal items to the new home, this was an obscene waste of money. Mimi and I were waiting for Mrs H to arrive, we had no idea what she wanted to keep and what was being thrown away or going to auction. When she did arrive, it was clear to us that she had nothing but apathy regarding the whole situation. We explained that we could help with the packing but needed advice on what stayed and what went to Stradella.

It was impossible for us to make those type of decisions. This was not going to be an easy task and I saw it running into days of work. I left Mimi with Mrs H to it and escaped to the kitchen. I had been told that everything in the cupboards and drawers should be taken out and placed on the counter tops. I laid blankets on the beautiful dining table, so I could lay out all the crockery and crystal glasses without scratching any of the table top. After that I went back to Mrs H's bedroom, where she had stuffed all her make-up, perfumes and face and body creams into plastic bags. She told me to throw them or keep them if I wanted. Did I want to? Hell yes, I wanted to keep, thank you very much. It was enough make-up to last me a lifetime. Yeah! Her frivolous behaviour had finally worked out to my advantage. Mimi had been instructed to clear out Barron's old bedroom, again sorting into piles what was staying for the auction and what was coming back to the house. The girls were coming over after school to clear their bedrooms, I was really looking forward to that, I knew Paris would be her usual obnoxious self. If you asked her to do anything, she would always say she had a maid to do that.

As expected, the children were more of a hindrance than a help. Like their mother, they had no respect for anyone or anything. Paris was having nothing to do with packing, and was only interested in how her pet rats were doing at home without her there to feed them. Yes this was the latest craze, not cats or dogs or birds, or even hamsters. Rats. Lovely. Nicky pretty much had no interest in anything and she still hadn't forgiven me for leaving. So the plan was to take all the children's toys down into the basement and lay them out on the floor. All clothes including Mrs H's were put on rails ready to be priced. The basement began to look like Harrods at the start of their January sale.

There were dresses from Neiman Marcus that the girls had never worn, bought as gifts from the grandparents. Toys never played with, some still in the boxes. All the poor children in the world who had nothing, this was terrible, it broke my heart to see such waste. On the ground floor in a side room, Mrs H had set up a small boutique with all her designer handbags and gowns on display. These were not going into the rummage sale.

I went there every day and worked for around seven or eight hours. Mrs H's one and only job was to put prices on her clothes, handbags and shoes. We had no clue what she wanted for them, or what the original price had been. One job and she couldn't even manage that. She priced up her really expensive things in the boutique, the rest she just couldn't be bothered with. Needless to say, when the big day came, things were organised, I have good organisation skills. But priced, not a chance.

Now when I made the reference to Harrods I wasn't exaggerating, the house was full to the brim. Sickeningly full.

The estate sale was being held at the weekend and although this was my time off, I wasn't about to miss the results of all my hard work.

We were all up nice and early. Wendy had arrived, she too didn't normally work weekends and like me wanted to witness this crazy event. The estate sale had been advertised in the L.A. Times and with people knowing the address and that the place was full of expensive items, Mr H didn't want to take the chance of it being burgled. So he had one of his agents sleep over in the house, to act as security.

So, my first estate sale. I had no idea what to expect. Neither did the H's if the look on their faces when we arrived was anything to go by. The security guy called at Stradella and warned us that there were hundreds of people at the home. The electric gates were holding them at bay for the minute, but he did fear for this life. I couldn't wait to tell Mr H and we both laughed hysterically, not sure if it was out of terror or anticipation.

When we arrived and saw the masses of people pushing and shoving to get through the electric gates, realisation hit us all at once. We were so understaffed for this event. The store was open for business so we couldn't recruit anyone from there. Before we dared to open the gates, Mr H rang round friends to see if anyone could come by and help. He did muster up a few volunteers. They were told to come a.s.a.p., let's face it once those gates were opened, we were all going to be up shit creek without a paddle.

The children were told to take charge of the toy section down in the basement and it meant they could play shop assistants. That way they were kept busy and having fun. More importantly they were out of our way. We were all given money belts and briefed about the section we would man. Wendy and myself were in charge of kitchenware and dining room related goods. We both laughed until we had tears streaming down our faces, it was mass hysteria. We had no clue who paid for what. Because Mrs H hadn't got around to pricing anything we made complete guesses at prices. I went into the lounge and heard a man say to Mr H "hey mate, how much for this table?". He had no idea who he was talking to, probably though he was just working these for the day. Mr H was always stern and very stuffy and here I was witnessing this man having a really fun time, he had a huge grin on his face the entire day. He would never admit it but I know he enjoyed being Joe Bloggs for the day. So here we were in shop-lifters paradise, and I couldn't think of a more deserving family to get ripped off, than this one.

Mrs H was having fun too, she was selling all her clothes and not only making lots of money to buy new ones, but was also making room in her closet to accommodate them.

Mr H's brother-in-law arrived, he said to help. I soon realised it was a ploy to snoop at their things and to see what kind of money they were making. He was selling pieces of furniture to people and not asking Mr H the prices. So I told him what was going on with John and he watched him. John sold a table to a man for a lot less than Mr H had asked for it, there was then a tug-of-war situation in the drive between this man and Mr H. Mr H let the guy leave and asked John what he had charged. Horrified by the answer he told John to leave and he did, along with the money in his pocket from all the sales he'd made that day.

It had been a really long, tiring day and Mr H told me to collect up all the money bags so he could see how much we took, and put it in his safe. Paris was reluctant to give me hers, she felt that as they were her toys, she should get the money or them. I assured her that her dad had every intention of giving it back to her, that he just wanted to see how well she'd done. Paris was so gullible back then, I could tell her anything and she'd believe me.

I don't know the exact figure, but we are talking thousands of dollars, that didn't include the cheques taken for the high-priced items. I then had a nice surprise, he gave me a very nice bonus for all my hard work. I got paid and had fun, two sentences I never thought I'd utter whilst working for them.

Sunday turned out to be less tiring and it helped that we all knew what to expect. The mountain of items had shrunk as well so it wasn't such a case of having to have eyes in the back of your head. There was still a lot of junk in the garden, stuff that hadn't sold so well on the Saturday. This would all have to go at some point. The buyers of the house had been promised it would all be cleared. That included everything in the garden. At the end of the day I found Mrs H walking round the back garden pushing an old pram. She looked like a bag lady, no make-up and scruffy clothes, so I took a photo of her. She was collecting up anything she felt to be of value because on the Monday, a junk man was coming to take everything from the garden that wasn't sold or kept.

The old house on Sunset, after the crazy weekend sale.
Kathy decided to help clear up.

On the Monday I went to the house to sort items into three parts, sold, needed picking up, going to the store. The rest was to be taken and stored in the garage at the house.

I called Connie to warn her that she was receiving a delivery of furniture to the store. She had a fit, the store was already jammed to the ceiling with furniture. She had no idea where she was going to put it. I politely reminded her that she worked in a store that was owned by a shopaholic. So Wendy had organised a junk man to bring his van and take the stuff from the garden and a charity to collect any remaining items still in the house. There was a cleaning crew coming the next day to get the home looking nice for the new owners. They had one hell of a job to do there.

Things were relatively back to normal and I went to the office to pick up the staff wages. Now from past experience I knew that Wendy's suggestions had not turned out so great for me. More often had bitten me in the arse. I knew she liked me and hadn't intended for things to turn out badly for me, well I hoped so anyway. So let's sum this up. I'd been on the European vacation from hell and spent a New Year in Las Vegas minding not only the H's kids but their friends too. Wendy's latest ask was that I cover for her at the office, while she took a vacation, just for three weeks.

I only had to answer the phone, no typing or computer work would be involved. I knew nothing about real estate and this was a prestigious realtors, so answering the phones was all they could expect from me. I really liked Wendy and I could see that doing this for her meant a lot, so I let her talk me into it.

Whilst I had fun at the estate sale with Mr H, this was not going to be the same man in the office. Mr H the business man, was a whole other human being. Wendy had been his secretary for quite some years so knew all his little quirks, likes and dislikes. I didn't really know him at all. We might live in the same house, but his personality was very complex. The fun he had at the estate sale was a real shocker to me. Even when we went to Europe on vacation, he didn't seem to enjoy himself, let his hair down, so to speak. So what was he like as a business man, under stress. I was about to find out. Yeah!!

Three weeks would fly by, right. Similar to the European vacation, this experience stopped time. Three weeks seemed an eternity and I soon forgot the fun Mr H. This man was the boss from hell. So I was only there to answer the phone. Right. Typing letters and lots of computer work was involved. It didn't matter how many times I explained to him that I have never been a secretary to anyone, in my life. He still insisted that I have a go. He said if Wendy can do it, I'm sure you can. Wow, I'm sure if Wendy heard that she'd be over the moon, the respect he had or her overwhelming. He was his father's son all right, Barron had given me the same impression when I met him. Needless to say I didn't cover any more of Wendy's vacations.

The store was doing really well, and I hadn't been there for a while. What with the estate sale and then the office. I'd missed my friends and I'd missed the daily excitement of someone famous dropping by. I remember one of my first encounters of the famous kind. It was an amazing coincidence, there was a Beatle song playing on the radio, and in walks Ringo Starr. The Beatles always reminded me of my brother, he was a huge fan when we were growing up and basically still is. Beatle songs were played in our house all day long. So my first thought was to get his autograph for my brother, he would be so chuffed. I didn't think Ringo had noticed the song playing on the radio, so I made a comment to him about it. I didn't like the look I got back, I'm sure he thought we had put a Beatle record on especially for him. If he had paid attention, he would have realised that it was a radio station and we of course had no power over what they played. He wandered off round the store with his wife, and although he had been a little off with me, I didn't want to miss this opportunity to get my brother his autograph.

Mrs H had given us very strict instructions that we shouldn't approach anyone famous in her store. Well she wasn't there, so what the hell. I grabbed a card off the shelf and approached this very cold man. I got the autograph and absolutely no smile in return. I wanted to tell him what a talentless hack I thought he was, and ugly. How dare he look down his nose at me. Oh well, I had got the autograph for my brother and I wasn't a disappointed fan, I wasn't a fan of his at all.

I had a better experience later that week. We had a restaurant next door called Cravings, and they had famous people in there every day. So we had a pact between us, that if someone walked into either their place or ours, we would, if we could, let the other side know. This one waitress Molly, knew I was crazy in love for Rob Lowe, this from his Brat Pack days. She told me he was sitting at one of her tables and my legs went to jelly. So gorgeous. I knew I would be incapable of going up to him, and asking for his autograph. I didn't want to intrude whilst he was eating anyway. So what was a girl to do? I went back into the store and wrote on a card. I said I was a huge fan, and didn't want to interrupt his lunch. Could I please have his autograph. I went back to find Molly to give her the card before he left. I had another look at him sitting there all gorgeous. Goodness, I felt like a giddy schoolgirl. I watched as Molly placed the card on his table, a pang of disappointment in my heart, he didn't open it. Well not yet, anyway.

I had to go back to the store. Connie was on her own and if Mrs H arrived, we would all be in trouble. We had a gift-wrapping room at the back of the store and Connie would often have party favours to wrap for one of Mrs H's friends. So I couldn't leave the front of the shop empty. Molly came by and said she had given him the card but he hadn't looked inside, so he didn't know to sign it, what did I want her to do?

Now I sounded like a crazy person, I didn't want her to let him leave without looking inside the card, he had to know I wanted his autograph. I looked out of the window and saw he was leaving, it was too late. Molly came back and was laughing. I thought that was pretty cold of her, until she handed me the signed card. So a lesson had been learned, there are approachable people and non-approachable people. Trouble was you didn't know the apps from the non-apps until you'd spoken to them, a little too late then.

My autograph from the gorgeous Rob Lowe.

So here I was seeing famous people on a daily basis and of course, loving it. There was a down side to this though. You know when you are at home watching the television and someone comes on you can't place. No problem, you wait for the credits to come up and voilà, you have a name. In real life there are no credits. People would come in the store, I could spend an entire day trying to put a name to a face. Sometimes it wasn't even a name that was needed. It could be a part in a TV series or a part in a movie. If they purchased something, piece of cake, you just looked at the name on the credit card. People rarely paid by cash even back then, lol. Of course, if they didn't buy anything it would be very frustrating.

On a rare occasion I would work on a Sunday, usually weekends were my time off. This one time there was a group of people standing outside the store. They looked like they had just dined out at one of the restaurants up at the Plaza. A family event, I guessed. They all looked around the store and it was evident they hadn't been in before, As this gentleman approached the pay desk, I was thinking how much he resembled Jack Lemmon. Until he spoke to me, then I realised his voice was very different to that of Mr Lemmon, and hadn't he died some time ago? He wanted to look in the cabinets at photo frames, and I obliged him. Very nice friendly gentleman.

A lady, who I guessed to be his wife, chose a couple of frames and after asking her husband for his credit card, came over to the desk to pay. She was nice and friendly too, so I decided to tell her how much her husband resembled Jack Lemmon. She smiled and said she gets told that all the time. So I smiled back, knowing I wasn't the only person who had thought that.

I ran the card through the machine and she asked her husband to come over and sign the slip. Who knew this would turn out to be the most embarrassing day of my life. On checking the signature against the card, I read the name Jack Lemmon in very clear letters. I wanted the ground to open up and swallow me. His wife saw in my face a realisation of my error and she gave me a lovely friendly smile. Yes, my face had turned a beetroot kind of colour. Unfortunately that wouldn't be my last faux pas. Opening my mouth before my brain is engaged, thankfully was a fault I did grow out of.

Carrie Fisher of Star Wars fame, "Princess Leia". She was a regular at the store and always very pleasant. Bob, our Christmas guy, had told me that she liked to have Christmas decorations up all year round, so he was always over at her home freshening them up. A little eccentric, I thought. We hadn't seen her for some time and here she was with a baby. She was with a friend and I tried to listen to their conversation so I could establish if the baby was Carrie's. It would be polite to congratulate her, but obviously not if it wasn't hers. I didn't have a very good track record of diplomacy so I needed to be sure. She called the baby Joe, so I knew it was a boy. She came over to the counter so I decided this was the right time. So I told Mrs Fisher that her little boy was beautiful. She thanked me, then added that it was a little girl. I hadn't heard Joe, the little girl was called Joley. Hey maybe she called her Joe for short, and that's what I'd heard.

While we are on the subject of embarrassing moments. Yes I'll hold up may hands, there were many. It was that time of the year, the nominees for the Oscars had just been announced. I loved the movies and would normally have seen or at least heard of them all. This year was different, I had been so busy in the store, I'd missed seeing the majority of them. Being a Brit, I was always pleased if one of our guys was up or an Oscar, especially if it was an actor or actress I liked. I knew Emma Thompson had been nominated so even though I hadn't seen her film, I was really pleased for her. The icing on the cake was seeing her walk through our doors just a couple of days later. She looked even lovelier in real life. I had to speak to her and of course I had this great excuse. I could congratulate her on the nomination. I walked straight over to her and said "I'm a huge fan and I just wanted to congratulate you on your Oscar nomination." She gave me a lovely smile and said "I'm really flattered, but you have confused me with Emma Thompson, I'm Emma Sands". I couldn't apologise enough and she was so sweet, she said she was very flattered by the mistake and wished she had Emma's talent and beauty.

Priscilla Presley was one of my favourite customers, such a sweet lady and never, ever condescending. Of yes some of these people were, usually the ones that were nobody's too. However this was a lady, and a joy to chat to.

Autograph from Priscilla Presley. Very friendly and chatty.

We had an entire twenty minutes long conversation once about hot water bottles. She told me how when visiting England, she would purchase dozens of them simply because she couldn't buy them in Los Angeles. She liked to take them with her on skiing trips to Aspen. She said, that a trip where there was snow and a log fire, wasn't quite complete without a blanket and a hot water bottle. I agreed. She wasn't extravagant but always spent a little money in the store.

Christine McVie autograph. Chrissy lived in an apartment just above
Sunset Plaza, so was often in the store. A very nice lady.
She was a vocalist with Fleetwood Mac.
Sadly she died 30th November 2022 aged 79.

Bruce Springsteen was a very quiet and shy man. He and his wife would always come in the store around Christmas time. He sat in the corner and she chose all the ornaments for their tree. Mrs H was always around when they came in, so I never managed to get his autograph. I did snag a credit card slip with his signature on once, though. Hey that counts, it's still his autograph.

They did spend a lot of money in the store. It was only at Christmas but hey ho, we are talking mega bucks. One year the wife decided to have us gift wrap individual ornaments for the children. She wanted them to unwrap them on Christmas Day and hang their own ornament on the tree. I thought it was a cute idea. They left the store and she ran back in to ask me to gift wrap a knight ornament that Bruce had said he liked. She told me to put in the card, *To Bruce, my knight in shining armour.*

I thought that was sweet.

Connie and I were chatting in the store one day, discussing who we would have on our wish list. On leaving England I hadn't imagined I'd ever have the opportunity to meet anyone famous, so I'd never really thought about making a list. Now those dreams were possibilities, so what the hell, I could make a list. Rob Lowe would be on it and now crossed off, yeah! Andy Garcia was a definite number two, I had fallen in love with him from watching the movie *When a Man Loves a Woman* with Meg Ryan. Then there was Mel Gibson, not from the *Mad Max* movies, but I did love him from his more romantic roles. Problem was, I couldn't imagine either of them coming into the store.

One weekend when I was still living at the H's, yes I did move out of their home eventually. I was invited to a charity event on the Sunday by of course the H's, and given that spending time with this family hadn't always turned out so well for me, I passed.

Now I was looking forward to spending a day at home with nothing but peace and quiet. It was quite late when the girls ran into the house and they were all excited about meeting the cast of *90210*. It was a show that I watched and quite enjoyed, but I was not jealous. I had no desire to meet these teenage heart-throbs in person, I did understand their excitement, this was probably the most popular teen show on television at this time. However my heart throbbed for more mature men.

Relieved I hadn't missed anyone of interest I went off to my room to continue my day off. My peace was short lived, all I could hear was screaming coming from the house. Obviously the parents had gone out to dinner and the kids were running amok. I could have ignored it I suppose, bit I always feared lives would be lost. Mimi was up to her old tricks of talking on the phone and ignoring young Barron. Nicky was up to her old tricks of tormenting him. Nothing new in the Hilton household. I knew Nicky just needed some attention so I asked her to show me the photos they had just taken with the *90210* cast. She was happy to do that and to tell me there was someone at the charity that I liked.

My heart sank. Who had I missed? Mel Gibson, that's who. The one time I said no to spending the day with them, and I missed my Mel.

When I went to the store on the Monday I told Connie how I'd messed up meeting Mel. I knew she wasn't really listening to me, she was too intent on telling me about her own exciting weekend.

Before coming to work for the H's, Connie had worked as an interior decorator. One of her previous clients had come into the store and they had become really good friends. This lady had lots of dinner parties and had invited Connie and her husband to one. No big deal, right.

Connie's family at her home, on Christmas Day.

Connie went on to tell me about the other dinner guests, and said one of them was Andy Garcia. Hey kick me while I'm down, why don't you. Connie had come with me a few weeks earlier to see *When a Man Loves a Woman*, starring said man of my dreams. It made it more intense seeing him in a pilot's uniform, we were both besotted. So in one weekend I'd missed an opportunity to meet number two on my list, and number three, Mr Garcia, had been stolen from me by Connie. Shit. Good job I loved her.

All was not lost for me. You know I said Andy and Mel would never come into the store. Well fate kiss my sweet arse. Connie was out the back gift wrapping and this was only a matter of weeks after her dinner party. He walks in, yes, Mr Garcia. Oh I wanted to play it cool, my whole being said don't fap this up Diane. He was with a male friend, and they were looking at the jewellery counter. Once I regained the feeling back in my legs I went out back to get Connie. I dragged her out and without saying a word, pointed her in the direction of Mr Garcia. She'd sat near him at dinner and had a conversation with him, so I needed her to be my wing man, so to speak. Would he buy anything? Would he ask me for help? Would my mouth work when I tried to reply? All kinds of thoughts were rushing through my head. I had loved his movie, so why not just tell him that. While I was debating all this crap in my head, Connie had walked over to him and was having a conversation with this man I loved. It was a very short conversation and he left seconds after. I was still frozen to the spot, it was then I realised I'd probably missed the only opportunity I'd have to speak to this man. "Spoiler Alert". My story didn't finish there. I did get another chance a few years later. You'll read about that later.

A girl came into the store one day dressed in what looked like jogging or gym clothes. I didn't recognise her, but she appeared to have bodyguards accompanying her, so I guessed she was well known. Her hair was in a ponytail and she had running shoes on her feet. Probably an athlete, I thought. Then a lady came in with her two young daughters and they seemed to know who she was. The girls hesitantly approached her and asked for an autograph. Ten year-old girls, really. They could go up to someone famous and I couldn't. Well not this girl, I didn't need her autograph, I had no clue who she was. Then Connie came in and said there was a crowd of people outside asking when Maria was coming out. Connie asked me who they were talking about and I pointed at the girl. Connie had no idea who she was either, but agreed with me that she looked sporty. She looked around and picked up a couple of photo frames, instead of coming to the counter to pay she handed them to what I could only deduce was a personal assistant. So Connie and I had no clue who this girl was, but she thought she was someone special. First impression of Miss Nobody. Condescending Prima Donna came to mind. So we were handed the credit card and after reading the name, we were none the wiser. I found out later who Maria Carey was. She was all over the tabloids by then. You couldn't pick up a magazine without her face or a story about her being inside, stories regarding her music and her relationship with Tommy Mattola.

Fun with all the gang at Ed Debevics. This is the restaurant where Monica from Friends *gets up on the counter to dance. Yes they really do that!*

One of our regular customers was Carol Matthau, wife of Walter Matthau. Connie told me that in her younger days she'd been a very beautiful woman, and an actress, I believe. You could see just how beautiful she had once been. Even though she hadn't aged well and looked a little dishevelled. It was quite obvious that she was on some serious prescription drugs and could barely stand. She would come into the store and always spend hundreds of dollars, so taking care of her was always a priority. This one time she came by just as we were closing. Connie told me to go and she would take care of her. I knew Connie had a long evening ahead of her. Carol was a sweet, sweet lady, who did her shopping in slow motion. She usually spent a couple of hours in our store so I knew this time would be no exception. She would walk round and when she saw something she liked, she would have us put it on the counter. After selecting a pile of gifts, she would then go through the process of eliminating some of them. This was all done while she was chatting about whatever popped into her head. When she was tired she would simply sit on the floor and surround herself with the items she had picked up. Like I said, it was never a quick sale with Carol.

Connie called me the next morning to say she would be late in. She said she'd had a very late night with Carol, I had expected that. I couldn't wait to see her to find out how many hundreds of dollars Carol had spent. Connie's face said it all. Carol had decided to make Connie her new BFF. She confided in her all about Walter's gambling problems and was stressed because he had gone out that evening with his gambling buddies. She then went on to say that he had played cards with these buddies the week before and lost a million dollars. Now Connie had a very teary lady sitting on the floor, surrounded by gifts and wanting to chat. Obviously Connie felt obliged to listen to this poor woman. Carol could certainly talk, bless her. All this would have been ok if Connie had made a great sale. However Carol left, leaving items all over the floor and purchased absolutely nothing. So by the time Connie had placed everything back on the shelves and locked up, it was really late.

That was the last we saw of Carol. I don't know if her health deteriorated after that, or if Walter bankrupted them with his gambling. Mrs H hardly visited her store anymore either. The novelty had worn off. It wasn't long before she was back to her old ways of staying in her room till lunchtime and shopping in Beverly Hills. She couldn't shop for the store anymore as it was overflowing with gifts, so she had to get her fix from somewhere.

A very beautiful woman walked into the store one day, with a very handsome man. I recognised her immediately it was Stephanie Powers. I loved her in *Hart to Hart*. The man she was with was French. I worked that out when I realised that was the language thy were conversing in. Hey I took French at school, I might not remember most of it, but enough to understand this was the language they were speaking. I had it confirmed a few months later when I read in a magazine article that they lived in a beautiful home in France. His name was Patrick De La Chenais and they had married in 1993. She was so friendly, one of the nicest people I'd met, so I had no qualms about asking her for an autograph. I grabbed a piece of Staircase notepaper and asked her very politely. She wrote, *To Diane, happiness, Stephanie Powers.* Such class and beauty.

My gift list for The Staircase

(213) 854-0176

Stephanie Powers, best known for playing Jennifer Hart in the TV series Hart to Hart. **Beautiful and friendly. She gave me her autograph.**

The same couldn't be said for the next person that walked through the door. Joan Collins. She came in with her nose so far in the air I wondered how she didn't trip over something. Too stuck up for me to dare ask for an autograph. What a difference there was between these two ladies personalities. Joan did buy a silver photo frame so when she paid on her credit card, I kept our copy of the slip with her signature on it. So I did get her autograph, she just didn't know it.

Because I only had weekends off, I treasured those times. If I could get away from the house I would, if the H's were away I made the most out of the peace and quiet of the home. If they were going away they always invited me along. I was always reluctant, past experience had taught me one thing, they always had an ulterior motive for inviting me.

So this one time they were going to Santa Barbara and invited me along. I declined for reasons I just mentioned. On their return I learnt that the girls had spent the weekend at the home of Michael Jackson, at his Neverland Ranch. Apparently Mrs H was at school with him and they were good friends. Could have mentioned that when you invited me. I think I could have managed looking after the girls at MJ's ranch.

The H's had gone out for the evening as per usual and the girls were going nuts in the living room. I could hear this commotion coming from the house. Even though my little guest house was separate from the house I could still hear the bedlam.

So they had decided to drag the karaoke machine out of the basement. Nicole Richie, Lionel's daughter was over and when Paris and her got together why would always act up. Fortunately Nicole's mother had sent a maid over to take her home. I guessed she was being naughty because she was rebelling about her parents splitting up, she was a handful.

I'd always wanted to have a go on a karaoke machine, but had never had the courage to sing ion public. This was my chance. The phone went and Paris answered it, I guessed it was Nicole complaining about having to go home. I was in the middle of a rendering of the *Greatest Love of All* by Whitney Houston. I heard Paris say my name and guessed Nicole had asked who the hell was slaughtering Whitney's song. Paris told me the call was for me and of course I wondered who was calling me, maybe the H's? I recognised the voice immediately, it was Lionel Richie and I realised he had been listening to me sing. He said I had a good voice. Initially he had called to speak to his daughter, not knowing she had gone home to her mother's. I couldn't speak to him. I handed the phone back to Paris and she was in hysterics, she thought it was the funniest prank she had ever played on me.

We had a grand piano in the house. No clue why. It had to be just for show, maybe somewhere to place picture frames. Nicky had a couple of lessons when I first joined the household, it turned out she wasn't musical and I hadn't seen it played since It made it's way over from the Sunset house and here it sat. I suddenly heard the tinkling of the keys and I knew Barron liked to play on it. So I went over to that side of the house to see what he was doing. There was no Barron. I went back to the girls and asked if they'd seen Barron and as I said it, he appeared on the stairs with Mimi. I asked her if she'd been downstairs with Barron playing the piano and she said no. The girls chimed in saying they had heard him playing with it. Now we were altogether I asked everyone to stay quiet. I wanted to see if we could hear the keys being played. Oh yes, loud and clear, someone was playing the piano. Barron should have been in ned, but Mimi wasn't leaving the huddle and neither was I.

A lovely piano that nobody played. Hey, it was great to stand photo frames on.

What was it about this family. Ghosts seemed to follow them everywhere. There was the one that roamed the garden at the Sunset house, supposedly the poor maid who drowned in the pool. Then there was the ghost at Barron's home, the girl ran over on the drive. Now we have a piano-playing ghost residing here.

The H's came home really late and when I heard the key in the lock I ran straight over to explain why we were all still up and huddled together in the lounge. I was expecting him to say how crazy we all were. Instead he laughed and said he had expected as much, he believed that having a ghost could account for him getting the house at such a good price. Was he just humouring me? Or had he just grown accustomed to living with ghosts. Whatever floats your boat, I would never get used to it. I raced to my room, which I add was only accessible through the room where the piano sat.

Paris was never really friendly towards me, but we had bonded slightly the night of the karaoke and ghosts. So I took that opportunity to ask her to get Lionel Richie's autograph for me. Shortly after I went to pick Paris and Nicole up from his Benedict Canyon home. I hid in the car, not wanting to meet him. I didn't want him to know that I was the person he had heard sing. The doors flung open and Paris ran out, but no Nicole. Paris reminded me that I had asked for Lionel's autograph and told me that Nicole was getting it for me. So out comes Nicole followed by her dad. He was holding a photo signed by himself and said he wanted to meet the English girl with the great voice. I was sure he was taking the piss, I know my voice sounds like a goose farting in the wind. Still I had my signed photograph, so what did I care.

Lionel Richie photo and autograph. Nicole got her dad to do this for me.

I'd been back in the Hilton household now for five months and I had managed to save quite a bit of money. That had if course been my game plan from day one. I had past experience with living with this family and knew it would only be a matter of time before I needed to escape.

I had made a lot of friends by now ands they were mostly up at the Plaza. Either work colleagues or staff that worked in the restaurant and shops close to the store. We were all one big happy family, that's how it seemed. Most waiters or waitresses were working at their jobs hoping to get a break, either in the movie or music business. A waitress called Heidi Fleiss who had previously worked at Cravings made a name for herself, running a more lucrative business. Her demise made all the newspapers in Los Angeles when it was discovered she was running, let's just say "a gentleman's club". Molly Shannon was a great girl, she always came in the store to let us know when someone famous was eating in the restaurant. She did stand-up comedy and we went to see her perform one night in Santa Monica, she was amazing, so funny. I felt she deserved to make a name for herself. She did, but not in stand-up. She became a well-known comedy actress. Nicole was a hostess there, too nice and sweet. The owners would walk all over her, giving her horrible shifts. Then there was Zachary. He would come by the store every day after his shift and tell us his life story. His stories did seem a little far-fetched, but were also very fascinating. Let me share his story with you.

Firstly let me say, this guy was gay as gay can be. Hell 90% of the men you would meet at Sunset Plaza were. So no shock there. This was West Hollywood and way too near the area they called "Boy's Town", to be populated with many straight men.

So this was his story. His name was Zachary Guggenheim, he insisted that he was related to the New York Guggenheim family. He attended private school in England and had met and fallen in love with another boy. On their return to America they carried on their affair but kept it secret from their families. Zachary didn't want his family to know he was gay, after all it was expected of him to marry a nice rich girl of similar status, preferably a family friend. So he did what was expected of him, married the daughter of his parent's closest friends. He had a fabulous extravagant wedding and went to live in an apartment in Manhattan, with his new wife. As luck would have it, his wife was away a lot at college, leaving him free to carry on his gay affair with the boyfriend.

Now doesn't that all sound like a catastrophe waiting to happen? Apparently not to poor naïve Zachary. Even with his wife's college days coming to an end, he still thought he could carry on the affair. His wife would be at home all the time and would expect them to be doing things together, so how was he going to juggle this. He told his boyfriend that he couldn't see him as much now the wife was back in the picture. He wasn't happy with the situation, insisting that Zachary tell her the truth and get a divorce.

The wife had already grown suspicious. She knew something was not quite right with their marriage. When she confronted him about it, he told her he was gay and not in love with her. It was getting near to Christmas and not wanting to cause a family rift at that time of the year, they made a joint decision that nothing would be announced until after the New Year. His wife also agreed not to tell either family that he was gay. Christmas came and went and they were walking their dog through the streets of Manhattan, discussing how and when they were going to tell their families about their break-up. Then tragedy struck.

A speeding car that was out of control, mounted the sidewalk and crushed his wife. She was rushed to hospital and later died in the emergency room.

Zachary was devastated, overcome with grief he hid himself away for several weeks. He didn't want to see or speak to anybody, this included the boyfriend. Time passed by and the boyfriend got really angry at the situation, so he decided to move the grieving process on by outing Zachary to his sister. Not a wise move. The sister in turn decides to tell the entire family. When confronted he admits to the break-up of his marriage, but denies being gay.

His life was a mess and for some insane reason he was blaming himself for his wife's death. He decided to leave New York, initially for just a short time while he got his heart and head together. His wife dying had left a big void in his life and he was trying to make sense of it all. He was questioning his sexuality, was he really gay? Or were the feelings he had for his deceased wife real love. He hadn't thought that he might be bi-sexual, well not until now.

He was really nervous about returning, having no idea what was being said about him. When he left, his family were barely speaking to him and the friends he had all belonged to this inner circle, a circle of money and snobbery. Anyway he felt ready, enough soul searching and emotional torment, he would face the music. He had no idea that his life was about to take yet another turn for the worse. The boyfriend had felt so bereft, he had taken his own life. He had taken a gun and blown his brains out. So Zachary now had the deaths of two people he loved on his conscience. Could his life get any worse? Of course it could.

The sister persuaded the family that not only was he gay, but that he had been the reason this poor young man had taken his own life. So Zachary ran away from his troubles, he couldn't stand the thought of having to face his family's questioning.

So this was his story, true, sad or a pile of poo. Who could tell, everyone in La La Land had a story, no one could tell which ones were made up. You have to admit, if this was a mad- up story, it would make a great movie. This young man now worked at Cravings as a waiter and was a million miles away from the rich lifestyle he once knew.

Once he finished work he would come in the back of our store for a chat, this was when he told us his remarkable story. Connie liked Zachary, she felt sorry for him and believed his story, I still juggled with it in my head, fact or fantasy? She told me one day that her and Zachary had been talking about my Green Card problem and that he had suggested I marry him. It seemed like a crazy idea at first, then after several weeks I did think it was an option I could pursue. Once I decided to take it seriously the question of payment reared its ugly head. Surprise he didn't want paying. He wanted me to return the favour by letting him tell his family he had remarried, thereby dispersing the rumours that he was gay. Basically so he could win back some respect from them. I could do that. From the day I agreed to this bizarre set-up everything happened so quickly. Our mutual friend Bob lived in an apartment building near the store and there were some two-bedroom apartments vacant. I knew we would have to live together after we were married, these things were checked by immigration. Zachary organised the licence in Las Vegas. The chapel was booked and the deposit on the apartment paid. What a bloody fiasco. Everything was moving along too quickly.

I hadn't told the H's what I was doing, It was the weekend and we took my car. Connie and her husband Gus came along as witnesses.

The blushing bride wore white, oh yes I wanted to do it right. Elvis performed the ceremony, you laugh, we did have that option., Well we had the option of an Elvis impersonator. We swerved that option and went for the guy who seemed to be the gayest in the room. Next to Zachary that was a shocker. I was sure he had some kind of gaydar and would know I wasn't marrying for love. It didn't matter, I just wanted it over and done with, especially the awkward kiss at the end, hey a quick peck on the cheek should count. We had some lunch and looked around Vegas a little, we didn't have a lot of free time, the drive back was going to be five hours. Zachary was really quiet and nobody understood what was wrong with him. Maybe he had regretted his decision to do me this favour. What the hell, too late, mate.

Me and a gladiator at Caeser's Palace, Las Vegas. What a hunk. This was my wedding-day, I'd managed to lose Zachary.

The flood of tears that came later was a surprise though. Yes this grown man decided to cry most of the way home, and he said I was being mean to him. I had no feelings for this man, maybe a little empathy because of the hard life he had endured. So this side of him was really annoying and made me question if I had done the right thing marrying him. Was he going to be an emotional wreck? Did he expect me to have some kind of feelings for him? Too many questions were going through my head. I still moved into our apartment the next day, yes our two bedroom apartment. It was a big place, we shared the living room and had our own doors leading to our own bedroom. They were both en-suite which made it a perfect set-up. I left the H's a note telling them I was now married and living in my own apartment near to the store. I said in the note that I understood if they no longer wanted me to work for them, especially as I wouldn't be living with them anymore. This was my way of letting them know I wouldn't be at their beck and call twenty-four-seven, anymore.

They called me on the Sunday evening and told me they definitely wanted me to keep working for them. I was managing the store at this time, as Connie had stepped down from the position a couple of months earlier, due to health reasons. They still wanted me to be manager and said they would be giving me a pay rise. Big surprise. They went on to tell me congratulations, this made me cringe, if only they knew the truth. Well I still had a job, that was a relief.

Zachary didn't move in for a couple of weeks, he had some time left on his notice at his previous apartment. He had been sharing with one of the waitresses at Cravings and she confided in me one day, that Zachary was telling everyone that we had got married. I asked her if he was emphasising the fact, that it was a marriage of convenience. She said he wasn't, and that she felt he wanted everyone to think he was straight and that the marriage was a love story. Get me a sick bag a.s.a.p. I had two reasons to be furious with him. Firstly, I didn't want people to think I'd married him through love, yuk. Secondly, he shouldn't have been telling anybody anything. It was a private matter, a matter that I didn't want to bring any attention to. Especially as I intended to apply for a Green Card with the hope that it wouldn't be recognised as a farce, by the authorities.

So yes, we didn't get off to a great start. I tore into him about his indiscretions and he cried for the second time. Oh what joy, this marriage and this man would be a monumental pain in my arse, I was certain of that. How do you avoid someone you not only live with, but work next door to? Not easy believe me.

Living in West Hollywood could be fun, gays do like their parties. The Viper Rooms was at the top of our street, a club owned by Johnny Depp and because it was owned by such an A lister, and because it was well known as The Club to hang out at. It was always busy and people would hang out outside, so it could be very noisy and disturbed my sleep on more than one occasion. It was the 31st October 1993 when I was woken up by the sound of sirens. Police and ambulance I believed. I thought It was outside our building which was very concerning, so I got dressed to investigate. Sadly it turned out to be the death of River Phoenix, who died of a drugs overdose.

As I no longer lived in the H's household, I had more free time, especially in the evenings. Going to the movies and eating out in nice restaurants with friends had to be my favourite pastime. Connie's daughter had a birthday coming up and she wanted to celebrate the occasion in a nice restaurant. Bob, the store's Christmas decorator around my new neighbour was invited, and as Zachary was in ear shot of the invite, Connie had to invite him too. Oh great, my darling husband was coming out with us. As if I didn't see enough of his happy smiling face all day. None of us wanted to eat up at the Plaza, lovely food but we had eaten too much of their food at lunchtimes. Connie knew of a great restaurant in Brentwood, she dined there before and only had fabulous things to say about their food.

The restaurant was called Mezzaluna, and as it was situated in Brentwood not Beverly Hills, we weren't expecting to be dining with celebrities. So it took me by surprise when I realised sitting on the table next to us was Mel Brookes, and his wife Anne Bancroft.

I didn't recognise the gentleman sitting with them, but Connie told me it was Dom DeLouise. This was a larger-than-life kind of man. I was a huge fan of Mel Brookes, so I tried to be discreet and get a good look at him. However, discretion was never my forte. I decided they were probably used to people staring at them, so why would one more peeping tom ruin their evening. Those were my thoughts and I was sticking to them. The waiter came over just before I made a complete ass of myself. Ding dong, he certainly took my mind off Mr Brookes. Gorgeous hunk, sprang to mind. Even thoughts of Zachary's presence at our table, which was annoying the hell out of me, had begun to mellow. We all flirted with him, especially Bob. Of course we all hoped he didn't bat for his team. This would have been a waste of this gorgeous hunk's looks. He was very pleasant and friendly, but in a *I'm your waiter give me a good tip* kind of way. Fair enough he was way too young and way out of my league, for me to be offended.

It was only a few months later than Connie pointed out in the newspaper that he was the young man butchered along with Nicole Simpson in her drive. This was all over the news, so we had all heard about it.

O.J. Simpson had been arrested for his wife's murder and there was talk that the young man we met at Mezzaluna Restaurant was having an affair with her. Of course I had no idea that this murder and the people involved would later be another part of this, my story. Watch this space.

Everyone loved Connie and she had lots of very influential friends, this had stemmed from her amazing talent as an interior designer. One such friend came into the store one day. It was the wife of the late Nat King Cole. They had met when Connie worked in San Francisco. They chatted for quite some time and Connie learned that Mrs Cole's daughter had just moved to Los Angeles with her husband, and it was them she was visiting. Connie knew the daughter also, so she told Mrs Cole to tell her to come in and see her.

Shortly after the daughter did come by and she seemed like a really nice lady. However I have a real aversion to people who make unwarranted noises. This lady had a snorting habit, that's the only way I can describe it. It wasn't just a sniff, it was very guttural and had a phlegm chucking down one's throat sound to it. I apologise for the detailed description, you had to be there. Or maybe not. She came in the store on a regular basis and apart from this annoying habit, I really did like her. Then we met the husband. You know how you build up an image of what someone's partner would look like. Purely based on their looks and maybe some of their personality. Well, Casey wasn't a beautiful woman or even very attractive. Pleasant to look at and a lovely warm and friendly personality. That's my candid opinion.

So when the husband entered the store we weren't expecting an Adonis. Bob and I both stood with our mouth's gaping open. Bob hadn't realised it was Casey's husband, he couldn't wait for them to leave so he could ask her who the hunk was. When Connie told him, he couldn't contain his laughter, assuming she was joking. Amazing personality aside, it was still a little hard to imagine this couple were married to each other. She didn't care too much about her appearance either, and he was immaculate in the way he dressed and groomed himself. He mirrored a gay man's personality. So the plot thickens. Kevin started to come by the store more and more. Connie had developed a great friendship with him and didn't want to listen to our theories, regarding his gender preferences, even though he was always in the company of really attractive young men.

Bob had a huge crush on Kevin, as did his best friend. Kevin was all they could talk about and although they had no hard evidence of this sexuality, they insisted that gay people had a kind of sense that helped them recognise their own kind. A sense Bob had made up, wishful thinking, methinks. When they were together in public, he did appear to be a devoted husband and Connie had been adamant from day one that their relationship was real. She said she had been to their home on many occasions and they appeared to adore each other, that he wasn't gay and she knew the couple better than any of us, so who were we to judge. Absolutely, who were we to judge. We all shut up about it after that.

Casey had asked Bob to go to their home to decorate it for Christmas. Bob secretly hoped that Kevin would be there, but expected it to be only Casey. He knocked on the door and waited some time for an answer. When it opened there stood a very naked Kevin, his excuse for being in his birthday suit, he was in the shower. Bob's first thought was, don't they have towels in this house? Second thought, Wow, this guy is so gay, opening the door stark naked. Even after hearing his story and having her son and daughter say they thought it true, Connie was still in denial.

Bib loved it when Kevin came in the store. I did too but for completely different reasons. He always had great stories to tell. This one time he told us what happened on one of his many shopping trips. He shopped at all the best men's clothing stores and was in his favourite, Maxwells, when in walk Mel Gibson. The poor girl behind the counter nearly fainted and turns into a blubbering idiot, this made Mel laugh. When he's in the fitting room this girl asks Kevin if he would take a photo of her with Mr Gibson. She was always prepared for such an event, having a camera under the counter. Kevin said he would, but that she should probably calm herself down a bit first. So Kevin hangs around waiting to take this photo for her. Mel comes out of the fitting room and the girl musters up the words "Excuse me, Mr Gibson, do you think I could have my photo taken with you?". Mel turns to the girl and says "Certainly not", and walks out of the store. Kevin is horrified, this man had a reputation for being such a nice guy. Then the door swings back open and there he is, laughing his head off. His arms open, he beckons the girl over to be hugged and tells her, no problem. Kevin takes the photo for the poor blubbering girl. Mel leaves and Kevin stays for a while as he realises the poor girl is hyperventilating.

Casey had a twin sister who lived in Florida. You would have though this was her only sister, as she never mentioned Natalie. Was there jealousy there, I don't know. They were identical twins and what was really funny, she had the same snorting habit. Casey and Kevin had a beautiful home in Hancock Park, quite an affluent area. I was invited to a big party there one evening. The invite was really through Connie, but I was pleased to be there. In the 90's there were a lot of these pyramid schemes going on, I mentioned one such scheme earlier in my story. Well, unbeknown to me, Connie had been hooked into one of these by Kevin and this was the reason I'd been invited. So this wasn't a celebration party, it was a ploy to get people to join this pyramid. I never pretended to fully understand the workings of these schemes, but I did understand this much. If you were not in it at the beginning, you were not going to make any money.

So I enjoyed the food and drink and didn't join up for diddly squat. I never imagined that would be the last time I would set eyes on the beautiful Adonis, that was Kevin.

Time passed and although we saw less and less of Kevin or Casey in the store, Connie was still in contact with them and kept me up-to-date on their life. She came in one day all smiles, she obviously had some really exciting news to tell me. She told me that Kevin and Casey were expecting a baby. Well this put the kybosh on our gay theory, or did it? I was still not convinced 100% and after I told Bob the news, he wasn't convinced either. Expecting is a funny word. With this odd couple it could mean expecting a baby to arrive in nine months via surrogate. Expecting a baby to arrive from an adoption agency. I know, let's be serious about this. Casey was with child and how it got there was always going to be up for debate. Was it Kevin's? I hoped so, a mini-Kevin, that would be one beautiful baby.

Sure enough Casey had the baby, and when Connie showed me a photo of the gorgeous little darling, there was no mistaking Kevin was the dad. So had we all been wrong about him?

Casey's sister had given birth around the same time so they were going to have a double christening. Casey's sister arrived from Florida a few days earlier to help with the plans. Kevin went out that evening to see friends, and when he arrived home the sisters were in bed.

He shouted upstairs asking the girls if they wanted anything from the kitchen. Casey asked him to bring up a couple of glasses of orange juice. So they waited and waited for the OJ's. Casey shouted down asking him, if he'd gone to Florida for the oranges. After he didn't reply to her sarcasm, she decided to go down and see where he'd got to, she thought he'd probably fallen asleep. Kevin was lying on the kitchen floor and Casey screamed for her sister to come and help her.

Sadly Kevin was dead. What was going to be a wonderful family weekend, a joyous celebration of new life, a double christening, would now be the saddest time of a young woman's life. A christening was now a funeral. Connie called me sobbing, she had been so close to Kevin. She told me she didn't know how she would be able to go to his funeral. They had grown so close and she loved him like a son. It was a blessing that Casey's sister had been there for her, through all this heartache.

The church was filled to the brim, Kevin was such an amazing person, loved by so many. Bob attended the funeral, he said, to give Connie another shoulder to cry on. He looked round the church and felt he had died himself and gone to heaven. It was filled with gorgeous men.

Casey approached Connie and told her she wanted a word with her later. Connie felt the conversation would probably be about what happened to Kevin and how she was feeling. Of course, she looked distressed as she approached Connie. However, Connie had no idea that the distress was caused by a conversation Casey had with one of

Kevin's friends. Apparently this young man had approached her at the funeral and told her that he had been Kevin's lover for over two years. He went on to ask her if she knew her husband was gay. I know Connie had always said we were wrong in our assumptions, but now she was hearing this from the wife. She asked Casey if she had known about her husband's sexuality, and Casey replied saying she had no clue. Then Connie thought of AIDS, this was a real problem in Los Angeles in the 90's. Because the store was situated so near to "Boys Town", and having been surrounded by gay men constantly, we all knew someone that was either living with the virus or had died from AIDS. Maybe this wasn't the right time to bring this up, but Connie recognised how naïve Casey had been regarding this whole situation.

Now the cat was out of the bag, so to speak, she felt she might as well ask her if she thought she should be tested for the disease. This was a shocker, Casey said she didn't need to be tested because she hadn't had sexual relations with her husband for the last couple of years. Then there was the question of the baby, was it Kevin's son? Yes it was, they had gone through artificial insemination. So all of this begs the question, how on earth could this woman think her relationship with Kevin was legitimate. How could she be so blind, to not see his friends were all gay. And to not realise that having sexual relations with your partner is a big part of a loving relationship. Of course they do say love is blind, and I have no doubt that this woman loved her husband very much.

The official cause of death was a heart attack. There were signs he had been in a fight that night. He had bruises and scratches on his face. So how did a very fit young man have a heart attack. The boyfriend told Casey that he had a drug problem, one more revelation. Poor lady didn't even know her husband took drugs. Did she know him at all? Now there would be a little boy who would grow up never having a relationship with his daddy. Very, very sad.

Not long after, I took over as manager of the store. Mrs H gave us all some news. She was having another baby. They were letting us know so that over the next six months we wouldn't be expecting Mrs H to do much work in the store. We all knew that wouldn't make a lot of difference, she didn't actually do any work when she was there. Sitting down, flicking through catalogues and ordering stuff, didn't come under the category of work. Did it? Anyway I was sure, that even with her being pregnant, she could still manage to shop, a task that needed very little effort. I wasn't wrong, now she was pregnant she had no desire to shop for designer clothes, as they couldn't be worn for a few months. So all her attention was focused on the store. She had to feed her addiction so buying for the store was her only outlet. It began to get fuller and fuller to the point of bursting at the seams. We still had a lot of crap from the house sale taking up space. So finding room for more gifts turned out to be an impossible task.

Connie was working part-time and had offered to cover the store while I took a few days off. I had a friend visiting me from England and I wanted to spend some time with her. We always had the back doors to the store open, mainly because the through breeze helped us stay cool, as we didn't have air conditioning. The doors opened into the car park an d some regulars would come in that way, or the staff in the next door restaurant would pop in for a chat. I had my bag out the back and in it was my week's wages and my driving licence. It was nearly time for me to go and pick my friend up from the airport, and I turned because I thought I heard the back doors close. They had, and when I went to see who it was, I noticed my bag had gone. I ran into the car park and noticed a very scruffy car, an unusual sight for the Plaza. I ran over and saw my bag on this woman's lap, without thinking I leaned into the open window and grabbed it off her lap. The car sped away and I stood there trembling.

Connie called the police and they scolded me. Brave and stupid were the words used, I believe. They told me that thieves and criminals, nine times out of ten, carried with them knives or worse still, guns. I could have died trying to retrieve my handbag. Well when you put it like that, I guess I did something very rash and very stupid. So a police report was made out and I went off to the airport to pick up my friend. I had a great time with her. I fitted in as many touristy things as I could. We went to Universal Studios and Disneyland. The rest of the time she spent shopping in the Malls and visiting the shops in Beverly Hills. She even spent a couple of days with me at the store, it was a shame no one famous came in while she was there, but I know she still had a great time.

In the beginning the store had been so popular, not just with the H's friends but with the rich and famous too. We had gift wrapped for

Hollywood Royalty. Now it was beginning to look like a junk shop. This family had a knack of destroying beautiful things, they had certainly ruined the ex-home of Jaclyn Smith. We had always sold such unique gifts, these people weren't stupid, they knew crap when it hit them in the face. I was working too many days now and getting sick and tired. We had a dozen boxes arriving each day, this was the Christmas period and unwrapping dozens of ornaments daily was no easy task. There was no space for Bob to put his trees. Something had to go. We convinced the H's to store some of the crap in their garage at the house. That way Bob could decorate his trees and the store could look wonderful, just as it did in the good old days when we first opened. Like I said, I was working six days a week and those days went from eight-hour days to ten or eleven hour days. All the ornaments had to be priced and there was just too much work for so few staff.

I lost a lot of weight. I was a tiny person to begin with, so losing more weight wasn't a good look for me.

It took a lot, but I had persuaded my mum to fly out and spend Christmas with me. She was seventy years old and had never flown before so yes, there was a lot of persuading involved. She was coming and firstly, I didn't want her to see me looking so emaciated. Secondly I wanted to spend as much time with her as possible. I didn't want to be working every day of her visit.

Mrs H had realised we were understaffed, and had from time to time sent someone over from the house to help. She had even thought it a good idea to send the girls over after school. They turned out to be much more if a hindrance than a help. So I had this dilemma, I didn't want to leave Connie without any help. But how was I going to spend any time with my mum. After I talked to Connie, she convinced me that my mum and my health were way more important than any job. So she talked me into resigning. Mrs H did not accept my resignation, instead she sat me down and together we mashed out a compromise. I would step down as manager and have less responsibilities. Having time off when my mum was visiting and work five, not six days a week. Icing on the cake, my salary was to remain the same. Yeah, this lady was human after all.

I liked her a lot more after that and might even go so far as to say I had a little respect for her. Well just a smidgen of respect, let's not go overboard. Mum had the time of her life. I took her to all the touristy places, Universal Studios and Disneyland.

We even enjoyed a day our at the L.A. Zoo. How did I explain Zachary to my mum, you ask. I simply told her we were room-mates, just friends. I forewarned him not to mention the marriage, my mum would have been horrified. Connie invited me and my mum to spend Christmas with her and her family in their beautiful home. My mum had the time of her life.

Christmas was over, my dear sweet mum had returned to England, and I still had a job.

It was January 7th 1994, and what happened that morning shook me to my very core. Five-thirty in the morning and for some reason I had just been to the bathroom for a pee, quite unusual for me. So I hadn't fallen back to sleep when I heard a rumble. This was followed by what can only be described as a freight train coming through my bedroom. Saying I was scared shitless, was an understatement. A feeling of sheer terror probably a more accurate description. The walls appeared to be moving and there was a sound of twisting metal. A cracking sound as the foundations rocked from side to side. Then came the smashing of glass as windows were lifted out of their frames. Car alarms sounding because the vehicles had been rocked. I don't remember getting dressed or opening my bedroom door. Zachary had already positioned himself under the door jamb. He told me to do the same. I asked him if he had experienced this before and he had, so at least one of us knew what to do. He also knew that there would be aftershocks to contend with. They arrived shortly after the main one and I hadn't had enough time to get over the first. My thoughts went immediately to my mum. Firstly I was grateful she hadn't stayed longer as she would have experienced this with me. Then I thought about the time difference. They were eight hours ahead, so mum would have the television on. It would come up as a news flash. I needed to ring her and let her know I was alright. For once I had impeccable timing, because after I had reassured her that I was alright and hung up the phone, it went out of service along with all the electricity and gas in the building.

Still more aftershock came and I was no longer comfortable staying in the apartment. Zachary grabbed a torch and we went out into the corridor. Residents were already knocking on people's doors checking if anyone needed help. Someone commented on a smell of gas and another replied that he had already reported it. I was terrified and although Zachary and I had been very frosty with each other of late, right now he was being very sweet and very helpful. I suggested we get out of the building. I didn't know how safe the structure of the building was.

We went back to the apartment and gathered together some valuables and headed outside. I couldn't get to my car because the gates to the car park were electric, so we just walked.

Connie had just moved into a beautiful home, within walking distance of our apartment, so I suggested we go there and check on her and her family. The structure of her home looked alright, but when she opened the door and I saw a very teary face, I knew she had damage inside. We gave each other a big hug and went inside. I was still trembling and the tears that streamed down my face were not just for Connie, I needed to get them out of my system. Her home was a mess. She had such beautiful things, a lot of antiques too, and many were on the floor damaged. A large cabinet had fallen too, because she had dealt with earthquakes before and knew that you should always use Velcro to secure valuable ornaments to the shelf. As they had just moved in she hadn't got around to doing that. Her husband Gus said that it would be best if we left Connie alone to sort things and he suggested that we should go up to the store to see what damage had been done there.

He drove us up there. When we arrived we saw a policemen peering through the window. Someone had called the police because they saw that a lit lamp had fallen over in the store and it was smouldering. He feared it would set the whole place on fire. Luckily I had my keys with me and we ran in just in time. Mrs H had always insisted we leave lamps on in the store at night, she felt that when people came up to the Plaza to eat, they would be tempted to look inside.

It didn't seem like such a great idea now. The store was a mess, stock laying everywhere. Broken glass and yuk, these bottles were once filled with pot-pourri oils. Well it might have looked a mess but at least it smelt good.

It took several days to get the store in order and it was pretty obvious that Mrs H had lost all interest in the place. It was now too full to put any more stock in and let's face it, buying stuff was really the only thing that did interest her.

In the beginning Arron Spelling's wife would buy gifts from us and have us gift wrap them. Then she started to buy the gifts elsewhere and had a gift-wrapping room set up in her home. Pia Zadora was another good customer, until she moved to Malibu. We had the odd phone call from her to say she was sending an assistant over to pick up a photo frame, even these calls had dwindled away.

Brace yourself world, another Hilton child was about to be born. It was time for Mrs H to give birth to another potentially spoilt brat.

The baby had been due on Mrs H's birthday and that didn't suit. So she arranged to be induced a few days early so the baby's birthday wouldn't clash with hers. What the flip.

You think that's bizarre, hold on to your hat. It gets more bizarre by the minute. Changing the due date, step one. Step two, madam has her hair and make-up done, so she would look glamorous whilst giving birth. Step three, well let me see.

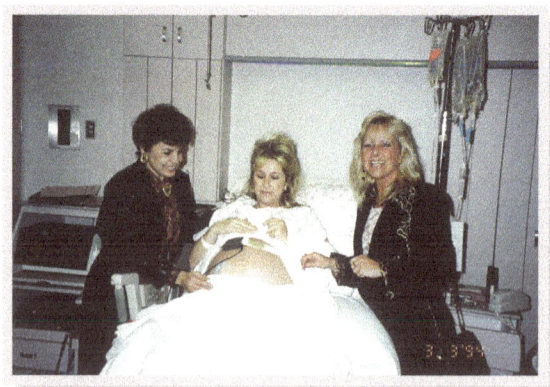

Me and Connie at Kathy's bedside in hospital. Bizarre I know.
Only in La La Land.

110

Connie and I were working in the store and awaited a call telling us the sex of the baby. Unfortunately I answered the call when it came in. I say unfortunately, because the conversation I then had with Mrs H had me laughing so hard, with tears rolling down my face, I couldn't convey her message to Connie for quite some time. When I had finally got myself together, I told Connie we had been invited to a birthing party. She asked whose birthday party and I said no, a *birthing party*. I asked Connie if it was an American thing and she said, not in her world. Evidently it was in the Hilton world. I told Connie that the party wasn't the funny bit, that Madam had organised the whole thing to be catered for by Chasen's Restaurant in Beverly Hills. We were eating a chilli buffet in the hospital. Obviously Connie thought I was joking, but hey, I wasn't. Connie didn't want to go and I had to persuade her, because there was no way I was missing this pantomime.

Waiting for Conrad to arrive. Chasens Restaurant, Beverly Hills catered. Really!

Dinner and light entertainment, yes a show was laid on. Could this day get any weirder? Mr H had previously videoed Kyle, yes that's Kathy's sister, giving birth to Farrah, her daughter. This was now being shown on the television in Mrs H's room. I walked in and when I saw what the show was all about, I ran straight back out. Kyle was there with her new guy, Michael Tuck, who was a Channel 2 newsreader. I thought he looked a little old for her. Guess she later decided that herself because after he had bought her a beautiful diamond engagement ring and a Mercedes for her birthday, she dumped him.

What was wrong with this picture? Surely if you needed privacy any time in your life. I'd say that was the time. It was one thing to have family around you, but half the people there were not family, hell they weren't even friends.

Kim was there and I was so pleased to see that she was still with John, the nice guy that bought her ex's motorbike. Pleased because he seemed like a really nice guy and Kim, for the first time in a long time, looked really happy.

Vanna White was there, she was famous for being the hostess on Wheel of Fortune. She too was pregnant, and I couldn't help but wonder if she intended to make her birthing day a fun and entertaining day for all the family. Judging by the expression on her face when the food arrived, I'd guessed, probably not.

Of course the father-to-be was there with the three children. I felt sorry for anyone in the hospital giving birth at this time. There were way too many children present and the noise was deafening. It was now eight-thirty in the evening and Mrs H was getting near to giving birth. At last people were thrown out of the room, just leaving the expectant mother and father, her sisters and mother in the room. In my opinion still too many people in that room, hey what do I know. I had just witnessed such a crazy turn of events, I felt like I was on a sitcom.

The new baby, named Conrad after another grandpa, was born quite quickly. He was cleaned up and presented to us by his proud dad. We had no intentions of hanging around to eat chilli, but we did grab a piece of cake on our way out.

Connie's husband, Gus, was waiting outside for us, and he had Bob in the car. Bob was very miffed he'd not been invited to this bizarre event. After all, he liked a good laugh. We decided to go to Mezzaluna, we hadn't been to that restaurant since the night we met the gorgeous waiter there, the one that had been butchered alongside Nicole Simpson. The food there was still amazing, no celebrities present this time. As we discussed the day's bizarre events, it helped us make sense of it all. We all needed reassurance that we hadn't just visited an alternate dimension, called the Twilight Zone.

Living with Zachary was getting more difficult by the day. However our relationship had thawed slightly, because he had helped me through the trauma of the earthquake. We had been married nine months now, nine long, long months, and I thought it time I went to see an immigration lawyer regarding obtaining my Green Card. After all, this was the reason I'd gone through this complete and utter farce in the first place. I did find a good immigration lawyer and made an appointment. Certain paperwork needed to be filled out, and on my return, I needed to take my marriage certificate and Zachary's wife's death certificate. I didn't anticipate any objections from Zachary, like I said we had been getting on ok. So his attitude when I told him where I had been and what I needed from him, was shocking. He did go a little crazy, I have to say. I reminded him of the reason we had married in the first place. Had he conveniently forgotten?

This was his reasoning, he had thought that as I had waited such a long time, I had changed my mind about applying. What bullshit was this coming out of his mouth, I waited for him to cry and say I was mean to him again, like the day of our wedding. I was bloody furious now, I'd lived with this guy for nine months in this unpleasant atmosphere and had nothing to show for it.

When I got to the store, I told Connie. She wasn't surprised, she said that after seeing him cry in the car, she thought Zachary's feelings for me were probably a little more than one should have in a platonic relationship. She also had a feeling that he was a compulsive liar. The waitresses in Cravings who worked with him, had been saying for months that things he said didn't always add up. They were sure he wasn't who he said he was.

Crikey, was this the reason he didn't want to fill out any papers, or produce his wife's death certificate? Had there even been a wife? Was his name really Zachary Guggenheim? I know it sounds like a mystery as seen on the BBC. You almost expect me to do, dun dun dun ..... don't you. Well this was true life, my life.

Had I been conned into marrying a man who was a fraud and a liar. It was looking that way. Well look on the bright side, at least I didn't love him, hell I didn't even like him much. Of course, this was all hearsay at this point. All these accusations people were making, needed to be proved.

So how were we going to do that, you ask. Well the waitress he shared an apartment with before me, suggested we look in his room for evidence. She said all the time he lived with her, he had his room locked. It made her feel uncomfortable, like he didn't trust her. As time went by she realised that he was just a very secretive person. She became a little obsessed and once let her imagination go a little wild, with thoughts of a dead body. Lucky for her he moved in with me, before she called the police of C.S.I. to knock down his door. She had definitely watched too many movies.

He kept his door locked at mine too. So looking inside wouldn't be an easy task. Everyone knew he kept his keys in his rucksack and that when he worked, said rucksack would be left out back. So the plan was to lift them, and I'd play detective, ok maybe I'd seen too many movies too.

My next day off was the Wednesday, and Nicole called me to say she had the keys ad would run them down to the apartment. What a bloody mess, there were papers everywhere. This guy was a pack rat and possibly a kleptomaniac. He had an address book which was full of Guggenheim family members. Hello, this was a light blub moment. The full names were written, not mum or mother, not grandmother or nan. This was written by a businessman listing his clients, not by a son listing family members. We found several social security cards with his name on them, but with different numbers.

He had shown us all photos of his home in Manhattan, and here on the floor were estate agent flyers advertising the same home for sale. Underneath a pile of these flyers we found a letter that had been sent by Zachary to the estate agent, asking for details of the property. It got weirder, we found numerous expired credit cards with different names on them. Newspaper cuttings everywhere relating to stories about his so-called family. Then yet another social security card, this time with another name on it, could this be his real name? This was all very overwhelming and I was beginning to realise that I was married to a complete stranger. Was I even legally married, after all if this guy's name was not Guggenheim, my marriage was a bigger farce than ever

I'd imagined. I copied down a couple of Guggenheim addresses he had listed, locked up and left. Eager to return the keys before he noticed they were missing.

I couldn't wait to tell Connie about our findings. She wasn't surprised, she had been doing some investigation work herself. She had some friends in New York and had been asking them questions about Zachary and the Guggenheim family. Evidently the majority of his takes had been proved fictitious. Connie was now armed with the address of the mum, so she wrote to the lady, showing concern for her son. We waited with bated breath. The reply came in the form of the letter being returned to sender, stamped with a postal note saying *Undeliverable, not at this address.* I realised that there was no point me living with this guy any longer.

My marriage was probably not even legal, and I was living with a liar and a con man. I went straight to my building office and put in for a one- bedroom apartment and gave a month's notice on ours. Zachary got mad and threatened to report me to the authorities and get me deported. I had a lot of good friends and after I told one said friend about Zachary's intentions, he had a quiet word with him and changed his mind. I never told him about the invasion of privacy, he just thought I was angry about his deceit over helping me with my Green Card situation. I'd like to tell you that I found out his real identity and the reasons he had all those bizarre papers in his room, but sorry, no, I never did. He moved on, sharing an apartment with a lady he had met up at the Plaza. I moved into a one-bedroom and never really thought about him again. Well except to get a divorce, in case it had been real. No one wants to get married years later and find they never got unhitched from the last one.

Maybe I'll see him one day in a magazine, headline reading, *Long lost Guggenheim son returns to his family after thirty years.*

Living in my new apartment was less stressful, but it still had its complications. At first I thought I was the only straight person who lived there, until I met a nice guy sitting by the pool one day. Not only was he straight, but from England too. In the 90's AIDS was a really big deal, as there was no cure and many of these guys would die. In fact many did. There was a really lovely couple who were very affectionate to each other in and out of the pool, they were very friendly and always chatted to me. Several weeks later the one guy was back by the pool and I asked him where his friend was. He told me they had gone back to France to see his family. I had realised his friend was French, and gorgeous by the way. He then went on to say that his partner had died there. Now I'm one of those people that don't always engage my brain before I open my mouth. So I gasp and say "What, in an accident?".

As the words came out of my mouth, I thought, you stupid cow. He didn't have to say anything, he could see by my red face that I had realised I'd made a stupid comment. The gorgeous French guy was one of many that disappeared from the building. This was a very sad time. I didn't want to judge these people, most of them become my friends, but I did stop going to the pool. I knew you couldn't catch AIDS that way, but still I started feeling uncomfortable living in this apartment building. I hated myself for feeling that way, but I did. My new found English friend was beginning to feel the same way. He had a guy living above him, who would come home all hours of the night, accompanied by very young men. The noises that came from the apartment brought him great consternation. So after many sleepless nights, he too had made a decision to leave. We both had notice to give on our apartments, mine was the longer one of the two, so he moved into mine when his expired. I didn't want to move too far away, because of my job at the store. But I did have a car of my own by now, so it wouldn't be too big a deal.

We got an apartment in Santa Monica, not too expensive, nice area. That too turned out to be a huge mistake, I did seem to make a lot of them. The neighbour upstairs moved furniture around in the night. Hell, I don't know why. Why did any of these people do such crazy things? My friend was away visiting family in England, when she decided to keep me up most of the night with her bizarre antics. So I went up there and banged on her door. She didn't answer, instead she called her big brother to come round and bang on my door and threaten me. The police came and charged the guy with threatening behaviour and on my friend's return from England, we moved out of that apartment.

Mr H was getting increasingly concerned about his wife's shopping habit and the lack of business being generated in the store.

It was a big store and to keep it filled with stock, Mrs H had spent a serious amount of money. Mr H didn't want to upset his lovely wife, but he had demanded a compromise. She could keep her store, but needed to move it to smaller premises. This way she could save face with her friends, she would show she wasn't a failure at being a business woman and still have her store, just smaller and with less expenditure for Mr H. The store was situated on the right side of Cravings Restaurant, and the new store was on the left side. So we didn't have to move too far. It was a lot staller and the majority of the furniture was never going to fit in, so it was moved to the house, to be stored in the garage.

We had a moving sale, and although the signs did say Moving Sale, the gossips still said we were closing down. We managed to sell a lot of the stock in the sale and I knew Mrs H would soon be buying more for the new store. We had lost a lot of our regular customers and Mrs H knew that. At first she thought about having another party, like the one we had with the first store. We didn't have the space and Mr H was not going to spend that kind of money again. After all, we are talking thousands of dollars.

Her solution was to host a luncheon at Le Dome. She would invite all her friends, especially the ones who had stopped shopping at the store. Le Dome Restaurant was situated directly across the road, at the Plaza. Her thinking was that once the lunch was over, her guests would accompany her over the road to see the new store. Then they would get to see all the new gifts for sale, and maybe she could draw them back as customers.

Well, you know I said the previous party had cost Mr H thousands. This luncheon was being held at one of the most prestigious restaurants in Beverly Hills. Madam wanted flowers to adorn the tables, along with party favours, and the guest list was as long as your arm. Check please! It probably cost as much as the first party, if not more. Now this was a business move, if pulled off could be very lucrative. I did think it was a good idea, if it meant getting back all those customers, ladies that had spent a serious amount of money on gifts in the past. It backfired, all that money spent on lunch and a handful of people came back to the new store. These women were not friends of Mrs H, and I found it hard to understand why she couldn't see that. Maybe she could and didn't want to admit it to herself.

The luncheon had achieved nothing, a very expensive nothing.

Not only had we lost most of our regular customers, business was getting slower by the day. The old store was great for Christmas, we had dozens of pre-decorated trees for sale there. Now there was not only a lack of space to display these wonderful trees, there was also no room to display the Christmas decorations, Bob, or Doctor Christmas as he was known amongst the elite of Beverly Hills, was also a no-show.

So all this added up to Christmas being a huge flop. More importantly it became obvious that Mrs H was losing interest in this new store. There was no room for her to buy stuff at the rate she had in the past. This of course was the reason why Mr H had wanted to move into smaller premises in the first place. Instead of Mrs H coming to the store daily and ordering from catalogues, this had become a weekly effort. Yes I would say effort, it was no longer a joy for her. Connie and I felt her lacklustre, it did rub off on us. The new store felt very claustrophobic and when we did have new stock in, it was impossible to find a space on which to display the items. On what were already very full overflowing shelves.

Mrs H surprised us all by being very hands-on with young Conrad, the latest addition to the Hilton family. I hadn't been around when Paris and Nicky were babies, so I hadn't seen the attention they received from mum. But I definitely witnessed a complete lack of interest in her taking care of Barron. So she was back to her old ways, luncheon with friends and shopping for clothes in Beverly Hills. We still saw the girls from time to time. A maid would bring them over to the store after school and they would play shops. The mess they left behind always looked like a tornado had hit the store.

I noticed Paris was really growing up, and dressed way too sexy for a girl of her age. It was scary how little attention she'd been paid by her parents, regarding the way she looked. She was definitely jail bait material. We used the same removal company every time we moved furniture. That had turned into numerous occasions so the removal men had become our friends. After delivering some furniture to the house one day, this young man came back to the store looking really troubled. I asked him what was wrong and he told me that Paris had been flirting with him.

He said that he was married and mortified by her actions. She had been bending down right in front of him, letting him see her underwear. Then pretending to help with the removal of furniture from the van, she moved in really close and rubbed herself up against him.

On the one hand he was flattered by the attention he was receiving from such an attractive young lady, but of course he knew that the consequences could be severe. He knew she just wanted attention and that if he ignored her, she would probably run to daddy and tell him the advances had come from him. If he did pay her some attention and someone saw, he would be in the same position. He was in an impossible situation. He had opted on ignoring her and now was really scared about the repercussions. I told him not to worry about the day's events, that I had witnessed Paris flirting on numerous occasions. I then assured him, that in no way was she going to tell her parents about her antics.

The customers had dwindled away, the stock sat lonely on the shelves and we were bored to tears. In fact a lot of the time we spent trying on clothes at the store next door, Boulmiche. My new friend Mindy worked there and would let us know when there was a sale. Hey, the Hilton's paid me ok but not enough that I could buy clothes full price from this fancy boutique. They had a sister store in Beverly Hills, this was the boutique Julie Roberts walked into in Pretty Woman, the one with the stuck-up women. I worked there later, you'll have to wait for that story. Anyway, back to being bored.

Mr H came in the store one day asking where his wife was. I told him she was shopping, and he said he didn't understand what she was shopping for, as the store was full to the brim with stock. I decided to ask him if he knew his wife was a shopaholic, ok, so tact was never my forte. Anyway he said he did, but he felt that by buying his wife her own store, the things she would buy would then be sold. Ergo putting money back in his pocket. This made me smile. This poor man had no clue. Buying a shop for a shopaholic was as bad as buying a Bar for an alcoholic. Once it was no longer feasible for her to shop for the store, she went back to her old ways of shopping for clothes. Again, feeding her habit.

Connie and I had made a decision that we would work there until after Christmas, then we would both resign. One last blast. We knew it had to come to an end. Kind of sad, end of an era. I would miss Connie, the girls from Cravings, and of course Mindy. I would miss the anticipation of someone famous coming into the store. After we handed in our notice, Mrs H still kept the store open for a while longer. It was a shock to see her working herself in the store. Something she'd never done before, I did wonder if hubby had insisted on it. I wanted to go up to the Plaza to see friends, but always had to be careful not to be seen by her, because she would have roped me into working there again.

The memories of working in the store will remain with me for the rest of my life. Great fun times were had by all. I hadn't gone to Los Angeles to meet rich and famous people. The thought never entered my head. Now I was reminiscing about the last few years, with fondness and with the realisation that my life had been an amazing rollercoaster ride, full of surprises, and this ride wasn't over yet. After all, I was still living in La La Land and anything could happen. A quote from the end of the *Pretty Woman* movie; the guy says "Welcome to Hollywood, what's your dream?". I was living a dream.

The difference was that my dream was never about becoming rich or famous, and that set me apart from everyone else. The wannabe's had a hard time. Chasing dreams had to be very painful, let's face it, out of the millions living there, only a tiny percentage would ever make it as an actor or actress. Or would succeed, having an amazing singing career. A life filled with frustration and anger. Kind of like a chocaholic, I know here I go with the holics again, so I love that word, sue me. Like I said, like a chocaholic being left alone in a sweet shop. Then you finally decide to make your move and steal a bar, you take off the wrapper, saliva dripping down your chin and you discover the chocolate is pretend, made of plastic. Unfortunately this is true of the people who live in Los Angeles, not all of them of course, but the vast majority. Nothing and no one is real, it's all made of plastic.

I kept in touch with everyone I'd met so far, that included Bob "Dr Christmas", he had a lot of connections and hello, I was unemployed. He had a friend who owned an antiques/junk shop, just a little way from the apartment building I'd lived in at Boy's Town. It was called

The Cottage and this guy Heinz who owned it, needed some help with running it. Needed help was an understatement, the guy barely turned up for work. He had given me a key so I could at least get into his shop. However nothing was priced, so even if I did get a customer, I had no clue how much he wanted for any of his stuff.

He had a lot of so-called friends that would hang about all day long. I say so-called because I was pretty sure they were ripping him off. The young good-looking ones would let him buy they coffees and lunch every day. We had a refrigerator in the shop and one day when I went to put a can of drink in it, I noticed it was filled with some serious medication, several bottles. That was when I realised that Heinz's lack of attendance at the shop wasn't due to him not giving a shit, it was due to bad health. This poor man had AIDS.

He had good days and bad and I hadn't mentioned to him that I had worked out what his illness was. His little friends were over and Heinz was having a really bad day, we all sat chatting and I decided to tell him how sorry I was that he had contracted this dreadful disease. He was a little surprised that I knew, but thanked me for my honesty. He told me that the guy he had contracted it off, was his partner. He wanted me to know that he hadn't been promiscuous, that unfortunately for him his partner had been, and had died from the disease a year earlier, leaving him with nothing but memories and a death sentence. I said I was so sorry. Then his two friends chimed in telling me they too were HIV positive so did I have the same sympathy for them. Bloody hell no. This was a man in a committed relationship cheated on by the man he loved. These two gits bragged on a daily basis about their conquests. They were getting no sympathy from me, in fact I was horrified that they were still sexually active, spreading this horrible disease across Los Angeles and America. How irresponsible.

I was even angrier with them when I asked if condoms were used during their sexual exploits, and their reply was that a survey had been done and it was discovered that 85% of guys living in Los Angeles had contracted the disease already. So they felt that there was no point in wearing one. I walked out of Heinz's store that day and never went back. I couldn't be around people who I felt were not only irresponsible but were potential murderers.

I hadn't thought too much about the store, so a call from Wendy, Mr H's secretary, came as a big surprise. Apparently the lady they had hired as a manager had been off sick for a while and they needed someone in there who knew what they were doing. I said I would get back to her, I needed to call Connie. We had both resigned together, I didn't want her to think I went behind her back and returned. Connie was fine with it, she just warned me not to get sucked back into working full-time again.

I agreed to a couple of days a week and when I walked back in, I couldn't believe the mess. It took me weeks to get it looking nice again, so I was really peeved when Wendy told me that all my hard work was in vain. The H's were moving to New York for a while and the store was closing. This time it really was a closing down sale, it took us a few weeks to get rid of the majority of the stock. The stock that remained went to the house. It seemed to be taken for granted that I would continue working a couple of days a week. I was really okay with that, the money was great so why not.

The night before I went to the H's house, I was sitting with friends in Century City, and one male friend commented that he wouldn't mind getting with that. A derogatory remark to make about a young girl. Then I saw that the girl was Paris and she was with Nicole Richie. They were giggling with boys and showing them their underwear. I gave my friend a warning telling him that she might look like an eighteen-year-old girl, but that she was definitely jail bait material. I realised when Paris was just twelve years old that she was going to be a problem as she grew up. She flirted with any make that same in contact with her, some old enough to be dad.

My new job was to help the H's pack up their belongings that were going with them to New York. I got the impression that this was going to be a trial period. Selling the home and leaving Los Angeles was a long way down the road. I did wonder how one family could accumulate so much crap, in such a short space of time. After all it hadn't been long since I helped pack up their last home. Madam's closet took a month to organise. Three piles, one for items going to New York. Two, items to give away to family and friends. Three, items to go into a potential estate sale, if at a later date a permanent move to New York was decided upon. Meanwhile the girls were meant to be packing their things, leaving a pile on the floor of clothes that no longer fitted,

Of course the girls hadn't paid any attention to anyone. They had been told not to take summer clothes, it was getting cold in New York now and the summer clothes should stay ay the house for now.

I hadn't had to deal with the girls for quite some time. Nicky had grown up, she had turned into a very beautiful young girl. Even though we had our differences in the past, she was very polite and showed me nothing but respect. Paris however was the same girl I remembered, impolite, rude, condescending and another word springs to mind. Egocentric.

Paris was at the age where she only wanted to wear her mother's designer clothes. Anything of her mother's that fitted her, had a designer label and of course looked sexy on her. So when I went to go through her suitcases to remove any summer clothes, any dresses she had managed to lift from her mum's closet were now packed in her luggage. I probably should have told Mrs H but I thought if she hadn't noticed the disappearance of so many dresses, she probably had too many to start with. Also said garments were going to New York and I couldn't imagine Paris getting away with wearing them in front of her mum.

When this task was all complete and they had left for New York, Wendy still had me working at the house two days a week. Making sure things were tidy, basically overseeing the place. That was easy. It had only been a few weeks when I got the call that things had worked out well for the H's and they were staying. It was now down to me and Wendy to pack up the rest of the house. We were left with all the dirty work, as per usual. Wendy appeared armed with packing boxes, tape and bubble wrap.

My job was to pack up everything that would be shipped to New York, and Wendy's was to organise the estate sale. Most of Wendy's job could be done from the office, she had the advertising of the estate sale to arrange and calls to Mrs H regarding prices to be put on the furniture. That left me at my own in the house, to finish the packing. Now I know I told you about the piano-playing ghost. What I didn't mention was the scary doll. Ok so you are now saying, what a wuss.

I know I have probably watched too many horror films. But I have a phobia about clowns and dolls. When I was still living there, I had a scary moment. I was doing some laundry and sitting on a chair in the laundry room was one of Mrs H's dolls. They were all over the house and I guessed one of the girls had been playing with this one. I had seen a film where a doll came to life and murdered everyone in the house. This was the only doll that really scared me, because its eyes seemed to follow you round the room. So I laid it down on the chair. On my return to the laundry room, I noticed that the doll was sitting back up on the chair and staring at me. Logic told me that one of the girls had sat it up, but truth was I was the only person at home that night.

Hello scary doll, we meet again. There she was sitting on a chair in the lounge. Those creepy eyes following me round the room. Realising I was not going to get any packing done in this room, not while she was sitting there, I put her in a black bag and out her in the basement. Now I could tell you that she got out of the bag and made her way back upstairs. However my story is not fictitious so I can't invent a creepy story for you.

She did however get left out of the packing boxes, that left for New York. This meant that when Mrs H came back from New York at the weekend and checked everything had been sent on, she discovered said doll, loitering in the black bag in the basement. I thought she would be angry that I had stuck it there, but she said she was pleased I'd thrown it, that it scared her half to death with its creepy eyes.

I explained that I hadn't meant to throw it, only put it away out of sight. She then told me that she thought its head moved on its own, she had turned the head away one night as it was creeping her out and when she came back in the room, it was facing forward again. So hey! Maybe the doll was possessed.

All the packing was complete. My job was done. I began to get a little nostalgic, this was the end of any era. I know I'd said some very detrimental things about this family. I know I'd said some very harsh things about Mrs H's parenting skills. But you know at the end of the day, I'd never come across such an exquisitely dysfunctional family. I had a love-the relationship with the parents. I loved them for giving me this opportunity and paying me quite well for the experience too.

The whole experience had been quite surreal, I was never sure if it was an American way of life, or a lives-of-the-rich-and-famous thing. I'll never know the answer to that. But hey, it doesn't end there, there is more to my story.

I had accumulated a lot of friends whilst working up at the Plaza. In fact, I believe I had more than I'd collected in a life time at home in England. One such friend was Mindy, she worked in Boulmiche, the posh designer shop I told you about earlier, the one where the sister shop was in Pretty Woman. Anyway Mindy had left to have a baby, so I hadn't seen her in quite some time. She always had a dream to run her own store. I knew she would be great at running her own place, she was an amazing sale person, she had talked me into buying many, way too expensive clothes at Boulmiche.

We had kept in touch, at least on the phone. She called me to ask if I would go and look at this shop with her, in Santa Monica, that she was thinking of purchasing. It was perfect. Not too big or small. Nice situation on a main street, surrounded by some great popular restaurants. Well Mindy bought it, and I was so pleased for her. She was now the proud owner of *Mindy's on Montana*. I went to see her and support her on several occasions and one day she asked me if I would like to work there a couple of days a week. She had been taking her little girl into work every day and felt she needed to spend some time with her at home. Hey you know what they say, when one door closes another one opens. This was my open door. Although working for the Hilton's had been very lucrative for me, I didn't want to spend all my savings, so a job working for Mindy was a great idea. She had great taste, so had bought some great stock for the shop, ladies and men's. The customers were not as snobby as I'd been used, which was a real blessing. I like down to earth, not condescending. My life was back on an even keel.

Then came the surprise call from Mrs H. She was in town and wanted to invite me to a luncheon at the Beverly Hills Hotel. It was to be a surprise birthday party for Wendy, Mr H's secretary. Well I knew there had to be a catch, I had never been invited to any luncheon before, without being expected to do or get something in return.

Sure enough there it was, I was asked to pick up Wendy's cake at Hansens on Beverly Boulevard. Normally this would be a job for Wendy, but of course she couldn't be expected to pick up her own cake. So that was the reason for my invite. It certainly was a surprise for Wendy, especially as her birthday had been and gone months ago. I not only had picked up this cake, but I had bought her a birthday card. Polite when attending someone's birthday party. I didn't know it was a very late birthday luncheon. I swear that woman would be late for her own funeral.

Still the Beverly Hills Hotel, not too shabby and a free lunch to boot, I wasn't complaining. I did notice that a lot of people were paying way too much attention to a woman sitting at a table near ours. Looking over a few times, I didn't recognise her. Then someone at our table said it was Geena Davis. When this woman got up to go to the ladies room, I realised she was over six feet tall and had bleached blonde hair, so surely this wasn't her. Maybe she was starring in a movie and needed to look like that. No I'm not crazy, I knew she couldn't make herself taller for a movie. She had to be that tall in real life, but the bleached hair, obviously that was achieved from a bottle. Anyway she looked awful, so I hoped a movie part was the reason for her look.

I don't think I've mentioned this before, but Mrs H was a little bit of a prankster. Humiliating people being her favourite pastime. She even made prank calls to family and friends on numerous occasions, yes she had played a few pranks on me, really too numerous to mention. I have to say I'm pretty gullible when I'm being conned. Anyway Mrs H knew from past experience that Wendy loved cake and that she wouldn't want to share her cake with everyone else. A sliver each would be our allowance. Hansen's cakes were her favourite, that's why Mrs H had bought the cake from their shop. The prank played was that Mrs H had called one of the lady's husbands prior to the luncheon, and told him to call his wife and demand a nice chunk of cake to be brought home to him. Because he loved Hansen's cakes. Mrs H knew this would enrage Wendy and it made her laugh thinking about how she was going to deal with her cake stealer.

Everyone at the table knew about the prank, except of course for Wendy. I did feel sorry for her, because the look on her face when the husband called was priceless. The wife even went so far as to cut a big chunk of the cake, and have a waiter bring her over a box to take it home in. It wasn't until Wendy noticed the tears streaming down Mrs H's face, did she realise she had once again been punked by her.

It was several weeks later that Wendy decided to take revenge and Mr H, who had been tricked on many occasions too, decided he would b ack her up. Mrs H was in awe of Princess Diana. So they plotted between them to trick Mrs H into believing that Princess Diana had been house hunting in Los Angeles, and had requested a viewing of their house. They knew she would be beside herself with excitement of the possibility of meeting the Princess. Wendy had warned me about the trick, knowing that I'd receive a call to spruce up the property for the viewing.

I did get the call and had real difficulty in keeping my voice sounding normal, as my laughter was brewing just below the surface. This was going to be an expensive prank for Mr H, but he felt it was well worth it, just to catch his wife out this one time. She ordered all new bed linens to go on the beds, professional cleaners in to clean and flowers were to adorn every shelf, nook and cranny.

The Princess would be arriving the next week, accompanied by her people and the stage was set. I had never seen Mrs H more excited, she was truly beside herself. I got a little nervous, it was one thing to prank someone, but to be on the receiving end, I wasn't sure she'd take it well. But hey good on her, she did take it well and she laughed about it. She was really impressed that they had both thought up such a good lie. A prank that even she, the Queen of Pranks, hadn't once suspected not to be true.

After the luncheon Wendy asked me if I was working, and I told her I was but just two days a week. She said that the H's needed someone to look after the house until it was sold. Her nephew was house-sitting the property, living down in the basement. They just wanted someone to go over a couple of times a week and make sure the house was clean and dusted, they still had a lot of furniture there, that hadn't sold in the estate sale.

The presence of the furniture did give a warmer feel to the property. Of course, the sprucing up it received from Mrs H because of the potential sale to Princess Diana helped, the new bed linens, flowers and plants. Unfortunately the majority of the flowers were on their way out now. But without the junk in the house you could envisage what a lovely property it was, and could be again with a little TLC.

The nephew being there was a good idea too, because workmen came all the time to get paint jobs done and to fix broken doors, etc. Oh yes, the children had done a good job of demolishing this once beautiful home. After a few weeks went by, Wendy called to say that the H's were no longer going to visit their property, not even at weekends. So the kitchen could be emptied of all food stuffs and utensils. Once this was done, a professional cleaning crew would be coming over.

As soon as I started to empty cupboards, I noticed small, brown droppings. Once I noticed them I saw them everywhere. I spoke to the nephew who confirmed that he too had seen droppings everywhere, he also said at night he heard the pitter-patter of tiny feet running over the floor. Why hadn't he told Wendy? I called her immediately and told her we needed exterminators in. Those little suckers needed to be gone. Now I say little. I was imagining mice, a mice infestation. Boy was I in for a shock.

I then remembered that Paris had pet rats that she kept in the garage, but assumed they had long since met their maker. Along will all her other pets. It seems that rats will mate with their brothers and sisters, they don't care that it's incestuous. So with that in mind and the constant supply of food they had had for months, those little blighters had multiplied.

Once I had thrown out all the food and cleaned up a lot of the droppings, wearing rubber gloves I might add. Then they laid their traps, we are talking hundreds of them. They were full every time I visited, not just with mice but rats also. We did think we'd got them all, there appeared to be no more droppings and no more traps had been sprung. Then this one morning |I went to the house and as I entered the kitchen, I saw what I thought was a cat trapped but still moving ion one of the traps. I ran out the room to look for the nephew and he was nowhere to be seen. So I called Wendy and told her someone had to come over. She came, she thought I was being a baby until she saw what was lurking in the kitchen. She then called the exterminators. This was the mother of all rats, a giant one, not a cat.

So now the vermin were all gone, the professional cleaners had been in and the house was sold. The furniture the new owners didn't want was shipped to New York. Now my work for the H's was complete. Or was it?

Another call from Wendy, this lady did not leave me alone. I'm just kidding, I loved Wendy. In fact I was in awe of her, she had dedicated her life to working for Mr H. She should have been given some sort of medal, or at the very least an Oscar. Mrs H had a friend, her name was Victoria McMahon, I had served her many times in the store. So I was a little put out at her attitude towards me, at Wendy's party. She acted like we'd never met. I wasn't having a warm and fuzzy feeling about this woman at all, but Wendy said Mrs H had recommended me to her, as she needed a personal assistant. Again it was just a couple of days a week, so what the hell.

Now I knew this woman was once married to Ed McMahon, and I knew he had moved on to some young slip of a thing. I then recalled an incident at the Plaza. The security guy came by the store one morning, laughing his socks off. He had worked the night shift and heard shouting coming from one of the balconies. He looked up and saw a naked man banging on a door, begging to be let back in. He shouted up asking the man if he needed any help, and when the man turned he saw it was Ed McMahon. The woman that lived there did finally let him back in, but not until she had sufficiently embarrassed him. We told Mrs H at the time and she did tell us that he was married to her friend Victoria. Looking back on that incident, I guess that woman was the young slip of a thing that he divorced Victoria for.

So why did Ed's ex need a personal assistant? Did she have a business or an acting career? Well it turned out, none of the above. It wasn't until my second visit to her home that I realised that she didn't actually need a personal assistant. Oh she needed assistance alright, but not in a physical way. The woman lived in a world of her own, one where she was still married to Ed. Saying she needed an assistant made her feel important. There was nothing I could do that she couldn't do for herself.

She wanted me to arrange her bills and list the cheque amounts that needed paying. However she would do it with me, so she could have done them herself in the first place. She had a lot of mail delivered daily and would lay it out on the counter top in the kitchen in some kind of order according to category. I learned that one of my jobs was to sort through the mail and place it in the piles accordingly. That was alright but by the time I left she would have undone all my work, meaning next time I went, I would have to start all over again.

Basically Victoria was a lady who had too much time, too much money, and needed to re-enter the real world. She was never going to achieve that living in La La Land, she was never going to help herself get back to reality.

What was it about this man, that she couldn't accept her marriage to him was over. I knew she was a flight attendant when she met him, so maybe being a nobody and then a somebody had messed with her head. This was not a good-looking man, He married Victoria Valentine on March 6th 1976, so she managed to keep hold of him for quite a few years. He was best known as Johnny Carson's sidekick. He was on the *Tonight Show* and *TV Bloopers*. An actor and a singer. So maybe his lack of good looks didn't matter, he had the famous profile and nice stash of cash. Amazing how some men can look attractive with those credentials.

They had an adopted daughter, Catherine, of whom they shared custody. I drove her up to his Mulholland home on a few occasions. He had a beautiful home and a lovely wife, Pamela. It was plain to see that he had moved on with his life 100%, it was only Victoria that was clinging on to her old life, where she was rich and married to Ed McMahon. Sad really. I probably would have felt sorry for her, if she'd had a warmer personality. She could change in a second, almost like a person with schizophrenia. She could be all smiles and happy, then just fly off the handle for no reason. I never knew which personality would greet me when I arrived at the house to work. Her life was one big charade, and in order to play this part she had to pretend everything in her life was fine and dandy and of course, it wasn't. This was one very unhappy lady.

130

She had me drive into Beverly Hills one day and pick up several dresses from Fred Hayman's. She had called on ahead and got the girls to gather together some garments that they knew she would like. They would be tried on at home. Victoria was a good friend of Fred and his wife, so there was no problem with her request. When I got back to the house, the maid told me that she would be taking all the dresses back the next day. When I asked why, she told me that this was usually the case. Victoria would have the dresses delivered and try them on at home, the next day they would all be returned.

Sure enough, when I returned a couple of days later the maid told me she hadn't purchased any of the garments, she had gone to her party wearing a dress she had in her closet. She had called one of the most expensive stores in Beverly Hills and had taken thousands of dollars worth of garments home, to try on. Was this part of her game, did she need to keep up appearances, with these shops and with her rich friends? I knew what her income was, remember I opened her mail. Her alimony cheque was $50K a month, which was for spousal and child support. Now I know that sounds like a lot of money to you and me, but believe me to live in that world and to live that kind of lifestyle, $50K is not going to cut it.

Again with the keeping up of appearances. At Christmas time she bought everyone she brushed shoulders with a gift. Every valet, every waiter and waitress. All the staff at José Eber's. She gave out dozens and dozens of bottles of wine and chocolates. Her reasoning behind this generous act, she said it was to ensure good service from these people. I believed it to be just another way of saying, look at me, I'm still important, I'm still rich. Now Victoria did live in a beautiful house in Beverly Hills, and I wasn't sure if it had been the marital home or somewhere she had moved to after the divorce. I hadn't been working there long when she told me she was moving, she said the reason for the move was to improve her lifestyle. Really!

Things became very clear when I went to cash my pay check. Victoria had been living beyond her means. Pamela, Ed's current wife, had a very successful business. She designed tuxedos for ladies. I heard that she was now so successful that Meiman Marcus and Sak's were both selling them. So I wasn't surprised when one of Victoria's so-called friends, told me that Ed had called Victoria complaining about the amount of money she was spending. He told her that she needed to get herself a job. That both him and his wife worked hard and he would no longer pay for her fancy lifestyle.

Given no other option, Victoria had to sell her home. Here we go again, I was helping to pack up yet another home. This woman was worse than Mrs H for hoarding stuff. The difference was this crap was worthless, and Mrs H's stuff was worth a fortune. I was asked if I could do some extra time, as the house had been sold and it needed a lot of work to get it emptied. By now I was being paid cash so I didn't mind the extra work. She hadn't found a home to her liking to move into, so she put her belongings in storage and temporarily moved into a hotel.

The house she did buy was down in the Valley, which made it even more evident that this was no longer a lady of means. The house was really nice and even bigger than her home in Beverly Hills. Edven so, living away from the glitz and glamour of Beverly Hills and her friends was always going to cause consternation. The charade was over along with her past life. She invited friends over but very few ever came, these ladies did not leave Beverly Hills, certainly not for the Valley. Maybe they thought they'd turn to stone.

Here I was driving down to the Valley two days a week, why hadn't I left you ask? Well in spite of her mood swings and her OCD with her mail, I did like her and I felt really sorry for her. I had noticed that she was drinking rather a lot in the day and when I asked the maid if she had noticed, she told me that Victoria was getting through quite a lot of vodka, like a couple of bottles a day. There was always a glass of orange juice on the counter that Victoria sipped during the day, so I tried it one day when she was upstairs and nearly choked on it, mixed in the juice was a copious amount of vodka.

There was this one friend that still came round to see her, and I decided to confide in her my worries about Victoria. I thought she could maybe help her, talk to her. This turned out to be a huge mistake. This was an English girl, and she had told me many things about Victoria's private life before. She had been the one that said she was living a charade. So I didn't expect her to go blabbing to Victoria about my concerns on her drinking.

I realised she had when I went into work a couple of days later. Victoria was really off with me and told me she now needed someone to work full time. Of course she knew I had another job at Mindy's, and I wouldn't take a full-time position. This was her way of getting rid of me without actually sacking me. There was no way Victoria needed someone full-time, quite honestly she didn't need anyone anytime. Not with her mail anyway. Yes I hadn't been discreet, I probably shouldn't have told the friend. You know what, mood swings aside I did like her, and only did it because I cared. She needed a good friend, someone who cared enough to be honest with her. Then probably later, a stint in rehab would have been a good idea.

I was now back to two days a week and a strange feeling of relief came over me. Maybe her craziness had been rubbing off on me. I really did feel de-stressed. I had made plans to go to Las Vegas that weekend with my friend, and wondered if I should postpone, now I was minus one of my jobs. I'm so pleased I didn't cancel my plans as I finished up winning $1500 on the slots at the MGN Hotel.

I never imagined working in Mindy's store on Montana would bring me into contact with famous people. It was always a given working up at the Plaza, because it was where they all met for coffee or lunch. Mindy was pregnant with her second child and asked me if I could work three days a week instead of two, as she was feeling very tired now. She told me that a lady had been in her shop with two children, and they had enjoyed playing with her little girl, Sophia. It wasn't until the lady had left that Mindy realised the lady was Robin Wright, the actress and wife of Sean Penn. The children had crazy names, Dillon and Hopper. Robin would often pop by with the children, hoping they could play with Sophia. Mindy told me that one time Sean was with them. Then Mindy or rather Sophia got an invite to a birthday party at their home. Mindy went with her husband.

My encounter with the Penn's would come later. Mindy gave birth to a second daughter, and I helped her in her store alongside her husband. It was this one morning, I had arrived at the shop and as I was unlocking, I realised I needed some sustenance to get me through a long day. So I locked back up, but left the lights on. As I was walking back I noticed two people sitting on the pavement outside the shop, drinking coffee. Were they waiting for me to open, or were they bums.

Turned out they were neither, in fact they were Sean and Robin Penn. They were hoping that Mindy was in the store with her two daughters, as their children wanted to visit. They looked just like everyday Joe's, Sean a little scruffy and a lot shorter than I thought he was. Robin had messy hair and wasn't wearing designer clothes. But even looking like that, with no make-up, she was a very beautiful looking woman. Not sure what she saw in Sean.

Here I was kicking myself because I hadn't brought my camera with me that day. I know, how stupid of me. Hey this was the 90s remember, not only did a very few people have mobile phones, but if they did they sure as hell didn't have cameras on them, this was way before the days of selfies. Missed opportunity and I didn't get another, they didn't come by again. Robin was mugged and the car jacked right outside their home on their own drive. They moved out the Brentwood area shortly after.

However prior to them moving I did have a friend of theirs come into the shop. It was Sunday, and this really tall man was heading towards the door, so tall he had to bend slightly to clear the door jamb. It was Tim Robbins. I don't know if it was my height that was bothering him, five feet nothing. Or if he was just knackered, but he decided to chat to me sitting on the floor. He said he was just killing time while Susan visited some friends of theirs. I knew the friends were the Penn's, because Mindy told me that Susan was at the little girl's birthday party. Susan of course, being Susan Sarandon, his partner. He didn't say much, just asked about the shirts we sold. Mindy bought them from a company called Jams World and they were made in Hawaii. So they were very bright colours and patterns. He asked if we sold many of them and I was honest, we really did.

I was very star struck and tongue tied. It's hard enough making small talk to a regular customer, but a movie star! Basically I just went to pieces and was actually relieved when he started to pick himself up off the floor to leave. I spent the rest of the day in a daze. What a surreal experience.

Maria Shriver, you probably never heard of her, but she was a Kennedy. More importantly, she was married to Arnold Schwarzenegger. I did recognise her, when she wandered in attracted by the Jams World shirts. She told me that her husband loved these shirts and had made all the staff at his restaurant wear them. The main supplier of these Hawaiian shirts had a shop right next door to his restaurant in Venice Beach. I didn't even know he had a restaurant, by hey ho, I didn't tell her that. Mindy was working in her shop more often now and encountered Maria herself. They struck up a friendship as they had been pregnant at the same time and the girls were the same age.

A few doors down from Mindy's was another Mindy, this lady had a health store and she told us that her business partner was a famous actor. When she told us his name, it rang a few bells. But we both felt that famous was a bit of an exaggeration. Mindy called me a few days later to let me know she had met the business partner and that this Jack Scalia was gorgeous. She was really excited and told me I had to meet him. On the days he visited his business, he would also pop into Mindy's. He loved to see her girls, he had two himself. Mindy said they were really beautiful. He had split from his wife and was living with the business partner and her girlfriend. That was a surprise, neither myself or Mindy had realised the other Mindy was gay. Especially as she was always gushing about Jack's looks.

Me and Jack Scalia in Mindy's Store.

A few weeks later I did meet the hunk and yes, he was quite gorgeous. I recognised him from having watched a lot of afternoon TV movies and a short-lived TV series called *Point Man*. Mindy appeared then and admitted she had pretended to come by and do some ordering. The reason, because she had developed a crush on our Mr Scalia. He was a very fit man and had jogged into the store, wearing shorts and a T-shirt. Be still my beating heart,

At Christmas I had brought my camera to work to take some photos of the girls and it just so happened that Jack came by. A Kodak moment waiting to happen, I think. I took several photos that day, some with the girls, but also a great one of Jack hugging me. I also had a few copies made and sent them to my mum and some friends in England. My mum was the most excited to receive one, she had been watching afternoon movies for years and had often seen Jack's face on her TV. She thought he was gorgeous too.

Our apartment in Santa Monica had turned sour. It was a lovely place, in a nice building. However we had the neighbours from hell. So time to move, and now we had the finances between us to move to Beverly Hills, not 90210 I might add, but 90212. There was the Rodeo Drive side of Olympic Boulevard and the other side, we now lived the other side. Hey, it was still Beverly Hills. Yes I was living the dream. I had leased a beautiful red Mazda Miata sports car, "midlife crisis methinks". Living the dream, it's a funny expression, because when you live in La La Land it all seems like a dream. The people you meet, the places you see. All the surreal moments that happen there. Everyday feeling like you'd woken up on a movie set.

]I was chatting to Mindy one day and she suggested that I do a couple of days where she used to work, Boulmiche up on the Plaza. I did like the idea of working back up there. I did miss the atmosphere, the people, the daily sightings of the rich and famous. She spoke to her old boss, the owner, and got me an interview. This was short and sweet and I didn't think I'd got the job, but soon received a call telling me I had. That was the good news, the bad was that I wouldn't be working at the Plaza store, I'd be working at their main store in Beverly Hills. Yikes, Mindy had warned me about that store, the owner's daughter worked there and she had a reputation of being the bitch from hell.

So this was the famous shop in the *Pretty Woman* movie. The one where Julia wasn't welcome. I loved the bit where she went back and said to the assistant, "Do you work on commission?". Big mistake. Of course they were actresses, so I knew I wouldn't have to work with them.

By the end of the day, I was wishing I had worked with those stuck-up bitches, they were way more pleasant than this little madam. She was rude, nasty and condescending. She even asked me if I knew how to colour co-ordinate. I told her that if I hadn't learnt at my age, I was going to be in big trouble. Christ, what can you say to someone who makes that kind of remark. I never met a more obnoxious human being. So her mum owned the store, she was under a big misconception if she thought I gave a rat's ass. The final straw was her embarrassing me in front of a customer. I took her to one side and in no uncertain terms told her that if she ever humiliated me again in front of anyone, I would knock her into next week. I left that day assuming I'd lost my job, after all this was the daughter of the boss.

I was really surprised to receive a phone call a few days later from the manageress at the Plaza branch, asking if I could work a day in that store. I was happy to, I knew the girl who worked there. She had been working there sometime, an Italian girl. I had a great day and it was really nice to be back at the Plaza, however my excitement was short lived. They only needed me the one day, as they had a girl off sick. So I would be working back at the other branch. There was no way I would be going back there to work. Even if my life depended on it. I took my money and ran.

I hadn't heard from Wendy in a while, I really needed to take some time out and go and see her. She had always been a good friend. Then just as I was thinking of doing just that, she called me. She asked me if I knew a friend of Mrs H, called Faye Resnick. I had seen her before, not shopping at the store, but I noticed she was getting some attention at Wendy's birthday bash luncheon. She had written a book and was signing copies. I didn't know who she was, so at the time I had asked Mrs H. She told me that Faye had been best friends with Nicole Simpson, and had written a book about their friendship. So this lady had written a book and was making money from her friend's terrible demise. Way to go lady, a true friend. Not! Only in Los Angeles would you find such friendship.

I'd watched the car chase and followed the court case, along with the rest of America, but apart from meeting the lovely waiter at Mezzaluna prior to the murders, I really knew nothing about the people involved. Not being an American sports fan means I knew nothing about O.J. Simpson either. Back to the first impressions I had of Miss Resnick, well they weren't warm and fuzzy, I can tell you that much.

Wendy assured me that she was nice and that she had asked for my number, because Mrs H had recommended me for a personal assistant position. Wendy wanted to check with me first. She didn't know if I had a couple of days a week free. Another one of Mrs H's friends, did I really want to go there? I told Wendy she could give Faye my number, no harm in that. I could still say no to her.

Faye called the same day and after she told me where she lived, this being within spitting distance of my apartment. Then telling me she just needed me a couple of days a week, so this wouldn't interfere with my job at Mindy's. I said yes. On the surface this seemed like a perfect job, two-minute walk, and two days a week. Now my only reservation was that potentially this could be another neurotic woman. It seemed to me that most of these Beverly Hills socialites had some kind of problem. Whether it be drink, prescription drugs, or just a shopping problem. Everything in excess and don't get me started on the fortune spent on plastic surgery.

Faye turned out to be a much more down to earth kind of person. I only worked a few hours and they went by really quickly. She had a really pretty daughter from a previous marriage, she too was really grounded, which was a joy to see after I'd witnessed the behaviour of all the other Beverly Hills brats. The job was easy, I would turn up and know exactly what she needed of me. She didn't breathe down my neck, she let me get on with things. I got more done in one week than I got done in all the time I worked for Victoria. Faye was in the process of writing her second book and needed me to simply open her mail. I sorted out her bills to pay and balanced her cheque book. It was clear this was yet another woman spending way beyond her means, there was definitely a pattern here amongst these women. Faye would receive letters from fans and those I dealt with. I enclosed a signed photo with a cover letter from Faye. I'd address the envelopes and stamp them. The other letters were from people asking for her help. These needed a more personal touch.

Her aim was to help people with marital problems, those who were suffering from domestic abuse, physical or mental. It was a personal journey for her, because of the way her dear friend Nicole had been treated. She didn't want anyone to end up like that. I had wrongly judged this lady at the luncheon.

I had known from day one that this was to be a temporary job, just some help to get her paperwork and life in order. When I arrived at her home one morning, two men were just leaving. They looked me up and down, and asked me what business I had at the premises. I told them I was doing some personal assistant work for Miss Resnick and that she was expecting me. I rang the doorbell and the door was opened by a lady I didn't recognise. She told me that Faye didn't want to see anyone that day and that she would call me later to explain. Okay, so men in suits asking me odd questions, strangers answering the door, way too much drama, way too cloak and dagger. When I got home, I thought about what had just happened. The men in suits were obviously policemen and the lady who answered the door could have been a policewoman. I began to get a bit nervous, had something terrible happened to Faye?

I nervously awaited her call and hadn't heard from her all day. By the next day I had become very anxious, so decided to call her. She apologised for not getting back to me, and for the interrogation I'd endured outside her home. She had been broken into the night before. That couldn't be the reason two plain-clothed policemen were at her home. She then told me that she had been in bed sleeping when all this took place. Nothing was taken from her home, but all the writing she had done, regarding her second book, had been wiped from her computer. It was obvious who had wiped the manuscript from her computer. There was only one person that would hurt from this book being published. It was never proved of course. Faye didn't feel safe in her home, so she went away on holiday for a while.

She called me when she got back and I told her I could only work one day a week for her. That was alright for her, we got stuck into the mail together. Her finances had suffered big time, and she asked me one day what I thought about her posing for Playboy. They had offered her quite a large sum of money. When she told me the figure offered, I told her she'd be crazy not to accept. She was very reluctant because she felt her daughter would be mortified by the prospects of her mum showing off her bits and pieces in a lad's magazine. Being teased at school would also be an issue for her daughter.

I told her that she needed to sit her daughter down and find out how she felt about it. Maybe she'd be surprised by her daughter's response, may be not. But if having her daughter's approval would help with the decision process, then treating her daughter like an adult and telling her that her opinion matters to you, would help.

She was really nervous about the talk, she thought her daughter might think badly of her for even considering the idea. But once she did pluck up courage and ask her what she thought, the daughter was really cool about it and in fact encouraged her mum to pose for the magazine. So Faye went ahead and posed. She was naked in the March 1997 issue, if you want to take a peep. Actually they were great pictures, not tacky at all. However, seeing your boss naked does make things seem a little unprofessional. All respect goes out the window. I know she did it for the money, and I know people have done worse things to help with their finances. I just felt uncomfortable being around her after that. It was a shame. Faye's calls asking me to work became less frequent and the working relationship just fizzled out. I was actually very relieved.

I always had work while living in Los Angeles. Maybe it was sometimes just a couple of days a week, but I always had some kind of job. I was very grateful for that. My dear friend Connie opened the shop next door. She had started up her own business, she had been making these dolls. The only way I can describe them is by saying they were a kind of voodoo doll. Not in any kind of sinister way, they were a joke doll. Made from materials and hand made by Connie. This business had taken off big time and she had been overwhelmed by orders. So this call from Connie was to ask me if I could help with the making of the dolls. She came over to my apartment and showed me how to put all the pieces together. I was a bit nervous that sewing would be involved. Sewing was not my forte. It turned out to be a stuffing and gluing process. Fiddly and time consuming, but easy work.

Even thought the H's had moved to New York, Mr H still had his real estate office in Beverly Hills. The business was called Hilton & Hyland, and it was Jeff Hyland that kept the business running. Mr H still had an office there and Wendy still worked there, as personal assistant to Mr H. I would call Wendy often, I always asked if the H's were moving back to LA. I never expected that Mrs H would be happy there, so I always imagined they would move back very soon. This one time I called her, she asked if I worked weekends. Their girl had left unexpectedly and they were anxious to get someone, because Mr H liked the phones to be answered personally. He felt it was really unprofessional for someone to call at the weekend and get a machine. I explained to Wendy that I just needed to have a word with Mindy, and I'd get back to her.

I worked Sundays and Mondays for Mindy, these being her days off. However Sundays were really dead, and she often paid me more than the takings for the day. I called her and asked if she thought closing Sundays would be a good idea. Her husband Mark had suggested it, but she was worried about upsetting me, taking a day's work away. She was really relieved when I told her about Wendy's proposal.

I went over to Wendy's office and told her the good news. She showed me how to work the switchboard and I started the next weekend. So now I had three jobs. Weekends at the office, Monday at Mindy's, and I worked at home assembling voodoo dolls for my dear friend Connie.

This was my life. I had a nice apartment in Beverly Hills. I drove a beautiful red Mazda Miata convertible, leased of course. I have three very interesting jobs and the glorious Californian sun. I knew the wannabees were having a hard time, because it's frustrating never quite getting that break, that makes you famous. However I was never a wannabee anything. I was living my dream, so why was I not happy. I'm not saying I was miserable, just discontented I guess. Bumping into Jack Nicholson in the supermarket or seeing the cast of *Friends* having lunch on Rodeo Drive had become very matter-of-fact. Life was one big blasé l excitement of meeting the rich and famous. When I started to analyse it all, it became apparent that my life was like a movie. Yes I was playing a part in a bloody movie, so what happens when filming ends? No wonder the people who lived here were crazy. I was heading in that direction too. I made a decision right there and then that I would give it just one more year and then I would write, The End. My story had lasted nine years and it was time to get the hell out of La La Land and return to the real world. My home, good old England.

I enjoyed my weekends in the office. Some of the agents would pop by for a chat. They would let me know all the gossip, whose homes were up for sale. Any celebrity listings they had. One agent had David Bowie's property listed, another had Farah Fawcett's. Kirsty Alley was looking at properties with a young hunk she was dating., he'd been in the hit TV series *Melrose Place.* Another agent, she'd just sold Ava Gabor's beautiful home. A really nice plant had been left at the property and the agent asked if I would like it. A plant from the home of Ava Gabor, hell yes. It had purple bows tied on it, when I asked the agent why, she told me it for good luck, and that I should also place a silver coin in the soil. Now I'm not saying that this crazy superstition has merit, but I did win another $1200 on the slots at the MGM in Las Vegas. Were these slot machines lucky for me, I had won $1500 previously, or were the purple bows the luck. Who knows or cares.

I was enjoying reading one of the gossip magazines I'd purchased on the way into the office, when the phone went. A man asked for Wendy and I told him that she didn't work weekends, and asked if I could be of any help. He needed to speak urgently with the Hilton's, so he needed a contact phone number for them. He had called their number in New York and had been given the run around from staff. I knew they were in Hawaii, but I had no idea where they were staying. Besides, I was sure they didn't want to be disturbed.

He then went on to tell me that their daughter Paris had run away from boarding school with a friend, and that they were headed to Miami for Spring break. The other girl's parents were very worried and angry. I took the man's number and told him I'd get back to him. I called Wendy at home and told her what had happened, she told me not to worry, that she would deal with it. I tried to imagine Paris hitching a ride to Miami. This was not a terribly bright girl, I imagined her being picked up by some lorry driver, her bragging about being a Hilton. Next thing you know Barron is getting a ransom call from kidnappers, demanding money for the return of one of his granddaughters. Would I ever get away from this family's dramas?

Like I said, celebrities didn't impress me anymore. Well I still hadn't met Mel Gibson and although Andy Garcia had come in the store that one time, I hadn't really met him. So they were still on my list of people I'd like to meet. Whether I meet either of them before my story ends, you'll have to read on to find out the answer to that.

One of the agents who always came in for a chat was telling me how she'd met Mel the night before. She had just split from her boyfriend and was out with a friend, when she remembered she'd previously met some really cute guys in a cigar lounge. So they went there and it turns out the bar was part owned by Mel Gibson. She them told me that he was there and chatted to her and the friend all night, she said he was really friendly and nice. Everyone was meeting Mel Gibson but me. Nine years in L.A., sightings of him everywhere, but never in my sight. I pretended not to be impressed, I told her that I really loved Andy Garcia. Then to add more pain to my bleeding heart she tells me that he lives near to her and that he goes into the same deli in the Valley that she goes in. Adding that he's always in there.

When I got home that day I noticed I had a letter from Mazda, my lease was coming to an end and I guessed they were probably asking me if I wanted to renew it. Another three-year lease was going to commit me to staying in Los Angeles and I had made this decision to leave in a year. I didn't bother to open it, but didn't throw it in the bin either.

Letter from Mazda. I had to read it a couple of times to let it all sink in. Because I was leasing a Mazda, I was invited to attend a charity game, which consisted of many of my movie actor crushes. To be up close to Andy Garcia, Kevin Costner, Cuba Gooding and more. What!!!!

It sat there for a couple of days and my friend said I should check it's nothing important regarding my lease. I opened it and read it. I stared at the letter and read it again. I was now staring and appeared to be in a state of shock, so my friend grabbed the letter from my hands and read it himself. The letter was inviting me to a charity golf tournament that Mazda were sponsoring. Sounds boring, right. The charity had been set up by Michael Douglas. There's more. The people playing in this tournament were, Will Smith, Kevin Costner, Cuba Gooding Jnr., Michael Douglas, Joe Pesci, Jack Nicholson, James Garner, Chris O'Donnell and Andy Garcia! The charity was the Motion Picture and Television Fund Foundation. I guessed I had been invited because my lease was nearly up and this was a little incentive to renew it. I didn't care why I'd been given this invite. I was finally going to meet Andy Garcia and a whole host of movie stars. Yeah!

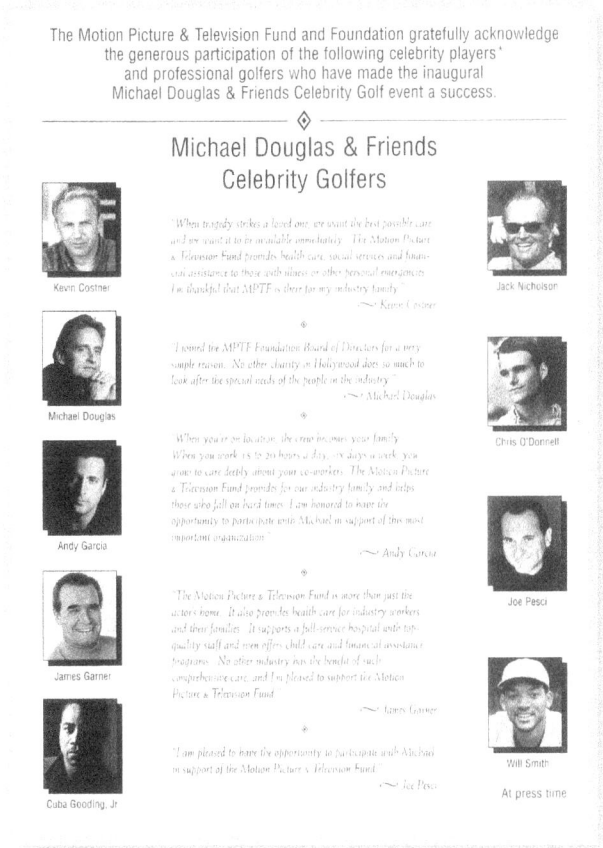

The Motion Picture & Television Fund and Foundation gratefully acknowledge the generous participation of the following celebrity players' and professional golfers who have made the inaugural Michael Douglas & Friends Celebrity Golf event a success.

Michael Douglas & Friends Celebrity Golfers

Kevin Costner

Michael Douglas

Andy Garcia

James Garner

Cuba Gooding, Jr

Jack Nicholson

Chris O'Donnell

Joe Pesci

Will Smith

At press time

The list of celebrities involved in the charity event. What a list.

I had to wait almost a month until the event and the day before it was raining. The forecast was for more rain that next day. Now I know you are saying, big deal, so it would be raining. But you see this was L.A. I know in Britain if men didn't play golf on rainy days, they'd hardly get any games played. Scotland, where it rains more than the sun shines, would never get any games played on their courses. In L.A. it's a different story, when it rains people cancel appointments, they don't leave their homes unless it's to go from door to door in the dry. No it doesn't rain acid but you would think it did, if you saw how those people act to a little bit of drizzle. So now I was panicking, would the game be called off. I waited till the morning and I rang the venue where the tournament was taking place. The lady who answered was really nice and laughed about men not putting off a game of golf because of rain. I wanted to say to her, well not in my country, but here, don't they think they'll melt?

It turned out that the little bit of rain that fell the day before, was a mere drop in the ocean compared to the torrential downpour that arrived that day. The car park was under construction and had become waterlogged, so we were directed to an alternative parking lot. This was quite a way down the road from the course, so they had laid on buses to take us to the event. Great start to what I had hoped would be the best day of my life. Slight exaggeration there.

I'd never even been to a golf tournament, so I didn't know what to expect from this one. All sorts of questions had mulled around my head the night before, the main one was just how close we would be able to get to the players. It turned out, very close. Apart from a television crew that was filming the event we could wander around at will. No ropes or security men. Basically, a stalkers paradise. I had the best day, the sun did eventually come out and the course was on a stretch of land overlooking the ocean. I got to chat to as many celebrities as I had the courage to approach. From past experience of the store I know some of them would be unapproachable. I was about to speak to Jack Nicholson when I saw him turn his back on a little boy, who was about to ask him for his autograph. I did think that was really rude, and felt bad for the boy. Then I saw how dishevelled he was. He had dirty hair and smelt like he hadn't showered in a week, he smelt of cigarettes and booze.

Kevin Coster, on the other hand, quite gorgeous. I hoped he wouldn't let me down, he didn't. He wasn't at all chatty but did give me his autograph and a nice smile.

Photo and autograph of Kevin Costner. I went to the event prepared. I had printed a photo of him from my computer, ready for him to sign.

Kevin in the background as I had just got his autograph, I don't think he liked me disturbing his game. But I'm a grab-any-chance kinda gal.

The real chatty guy was Cuba Gooding Jnr., huge respect for this guy now. He was so nice and friendly, he put his arms around me, and asked if I was having a good time, hey I was now.

Photo of Cuba Gooding and autograph.

I wish the photos had come out a little clearer. The golfing green was on a cliff overlooking the ocean and the glare from the water didn't help. This was in the day before selfies or camera phones. My little camera was not even digital, it was the old fashioned film-in type. Yes any millennials reading this, we didn't have camera phones then!

So where was Mr Garcia, my reason for living. I did track him down, he not only chatted to me, he let my friend take a photograph of us. When I handed him a photo to sign that I'd printed off a computer, he laughed and asked where it was taken. Neither of us had a clue where he was on the photo, buy hey, he signed it anyway. Then he gave me a big hug and moved on to play the next hole. Be still my beating heart.

Andy Garcia photo and autograph.

Another prepared photo printed out ready in case I had the opportunity to get it signed by the man. He asked me where the photo was taken. I laughed. I told him I had printed it from a computer, and he was baffled as to where he was at the time.

Me and Mr Garcia just after he signed my photo. He was very chatty and friendly.

I got the photos developed the same day at a one-hour shop. They were not as clear as I'd have liked, but hey, I'd had such an amazing day.

Game Boards. Kevin was interviewed for the televised coverage of the game.

Me and my Mazda car. I never would have dreamed that leasing this car would have given me this wonderful opportunity to meet so many celebrities.

The next day the Oscars were on the television. Garcia, Costner and Nicholson up there on the screen, made the day before seem surreal. I had been standing right next to all three of them hours ago and here they were on my TV, on the red carpet at the Oscars.

The lease was now up on my Mazda and I had a big decision to make. If I was only going to live in Los Angeles for one more year, a three-year lease was out of the question. I didn't need a car for work anymore. Mindy's had closed, my dear friend was leaving L.A. for pastures new, Hawaii. I would miss her but knew she would be so happy there. Her family had grown too big for their home and buying bigger in Los Angeles was way beyond their budget. They had found a large home in Hawaii and decided it would be a better place to bring up their girls. My weekend job at the H's real estate office was within walking distance of my home and the dolls I made for Connie were done at home. My friend and roommate had just leased a new car and he said I could borrow that whenever I needed, so I insured myself to drive that and returned my lovely red car to the Mazda dealers.

This was definitely it. The movie shoot was over, all the famous actors had played their parts. Mel never did turn up to play his part, but Andy and Kevin had filled in for him and done a great job.

The Californian sun which had once been a pleasure was now driving me crazy. Living with a timebomb under your arse 24/7. By timebomb I mean the thousands of earthquake faults waiting to connect up. Knowing that if these faults do connect, it will create the Big One. That's the earthquake that will hit with such magnitude that California will break away from the mainland. This San Andreas fault runs across the whole length of California.

This felt like the right time to say my goodbyes. While I still had my Mazda, I decided to take a drive down to the Valley. Now I'm not proud of this, whilst working at Mr H's offices I had access to names and addresses of residents in California. Well not me exactly, there was a site that the agents could access and I just happened to know the password to get into this site. So armed with the address of a Mr Garcia, I decided I would go look at where he lived. There was no sign of life at the home and I did sit in the car for an hour or so. Then the realisation hit me, I had become a stalker. I would be in the tabloids next day. Headlines, crazy woman stalks Andy Garcia. Yikes. I didn't go back, honest.

New Year's Eve was here, we had dinner at a fantastic Beverly Hills restaurant. Celebrating the new Millennium. I had spent the 90's in Los Angeles and it had been one hell of a ride. I wanted to be home in time to celebrate my mum's 77th birthday, that was on April 7th. I hadn't told her I was coming home, I wanted it to be a surprise. She hadn't seen me for five years.

I'd like to say this is the end of my story, living in La La Land, because this would be a happy ending and everyone loves a happy ending. This, however, is not the case.

I'd been enjoying playing a tourist, visiting or revisiting all the fun places Los Angeles had to offer. My friend needed me to drive him to work, then I could have his car for the day. I came up to the traffic lights and they were on green, so I drove straight over Olympic Boulevard. A car decided to turn left, smashing into the side of our car. I pulled over just outside the Beverly Hills High School, and hurried after them in case they drove away.

A young girl gets out the car and starts hurling abuse at me, and this is not even the driver of the vehicle, she's the passenger. We are standing outside a park and the ranger arrives out of nowhere and although he'd not witnessed the accident, he decides to interfere in the matter. I was very shaken up and adding insult to injury, the language coming out of this young lady's mouth was horrific. I was getting really angry now, everyone shouting, accusations flying everywhere. It was clearly this girl's fault, so when she called me a crazy bitch that didn't know how to drive, I just flipped.

My friend had called the police. It was looking like an impossible situation, all we needed were the insurance details from the driver, this passenger was not acting rational at all. I kept asking her to get back in the car so I could deal with the driver, but she hadn't hurled enough abuse at me. I went to put my hand over her mouth to shut her up, she moved and I scratched her neck with my fingernails. Now instead of my hands being over her mouth, they were round her neck. She started shouting to the park ranger that the bitch had tried to strangle her. He wasn't in a position to see what was going on, but decided to call the police anyway. So, two lots of police arrived.

Here begins my nightmare. The police interviewed us all individually and then came back and told me they were arresting me. If I hadn't been in so much shock, I probably would have cried. They let Dean take my handbag and my jewellery and then they handcuffed me. It's not easy for me to tell this story, as I still look back on that day with consternation. Here I was sitting in the back of a police car being taken to the Beverly Hills police station. On arrival I was told to remove my shoes, this was in case I kicked one of the officers. Here I stood, five foot tall, 102lbs., wearing an Armani suit. Did I really look like someone who was going to kick off?

They handed me a pair of yellow slip-on shoes to place on my now bare feet. Looking down I noticed they had a smiley face on them, someone had a sense of humour. Not me, all my humour and indeed senses had left my body. It gets worse, I had to have a mug-shot taken, finger and thumb prints. Thankfully the officer charging me seemed really nice, and I'm sure sensed I wasn't a real criminal. He apologised for having to put me through in a cell while my papers were being processed. He even asked me if I wanted something to drink.

I was locked up for three hours, probably the longest three hours of my life. There was a friendly face waiting for me when I was released and when he hugged me, all my feelings welled up and I burst into tears. What a day, what a nightmare. If only I'd left after the golf tournament, then I'd only have good memories to cherish.

The car was barely driveable, although we did manage to get it back to the dealership and dealt with the insurance claim. We won the case, because I had driven over on a green light and she had turned left into our car, she had made an illegal turn. She should have given way to oncoming traffic. She only had her name on her dad's insurance and he was really angry. Even more so when we claimed for whiplash. Dean had problems from standing all day cutting hair and I had an old shoulder injury from a bad ride on a ride at a fair. So because of the stress she had caused me, we went to some very expensive chiropractors in Beverly Hills and had several nice sessions there.

I still had a court case pending, which was bringing me down. I was found guilty, a photo had been taken of the girl's scratched neck, so they had evidence of assault. The girl had just turned eighteen and the judge said if she had been seventeen and a minor, I would be given a custodial sentence. Thank God she'd had a birthday. I got forty hours community service and a $400 fine. When I looked at the list of places

I could do the community service, I saw that I could work at a charity shop. It just so happened that I went into this cancer charity shop on a daily basis. I'd picked up some great secondhand designer clothes in there, and I knew the ladies really well. I'd even told a couple of them what had happened to me. The manageress was very happy to let me work out my forty hours there. In fact she signed off my paperwork before I'd even completed the full time. So it wasn't all bad. Yes, if I'd have left sooner, I'd have had my happy ending but you know what, I still had the time of my life.

That's where my original manuscript finished. But I'm writing this, nineteen years on, and I would like to tell you how things turned out for me and the people who played a part in my story. Hopefully I left out the boring bits.

Adjusting to normal life, that was never going to be easy. I had the big birthday surprise for my mum, that went really well. Tears all round. She thought she was going for a birthday dinner with my brother and his wife. Then I turned up and made her day, she hadn't seen me in five years, and telling her I was home for good made her even happier.

When I told her I was staying I had my fingers crossed, was I telling her a lie? I couldn't be sure that I'd be able to settle for little old Norwich, could I settle for a mundane life. Gone would be the prospects of seeing movie stars or anyone famous ever again. Well I had to give it a try. The key was to keep telling myself these people were real people, warm and friendly. They didn't befriend you simply to see what you could do for them. They didn't make plans with you and turn up an hour late, with no excuse. Real people and I had loved them before I went to Los Angeles, and I would love them again.

I had all these stories to tell about my experiences and once I had told family and friends, the memories began to fade. When I told new friends or acquaintances, I could tell by the look on their faces that they thought I was telling them lies, crazy made-up stories. I couldn't blame them, if someone was telling me the same stories I'd think the same. So when the expression on their face read, "can you believe this crap", I understandably clammed up and quickly changed the subject.

My friend Connie from my previous life had loved hearing my stories from the Hilton household. When I got to the store in the mornings, I always had a story to tell her and she always said, you should write a book. At this point I stopped talking about my experiences and had wondered if I would in time forget them all. So maybe writing a book would be a good idea. It started off, just being a diary of events. Then I purchased a computer and the diary turned into a manuscript.

I'd been home eight months now and really missed my friends, yes I did have some real ones. My friend still lived in our apartment in Beverly Hills, so I had somewhere to stay if I went for a visit. I hadn't been looking for work yet, just chilling out. So now was the time to visit before I was tied down with work commitments. I had to spend Christmas with mum, the first for many years. But shortly after, I did go out there for six weeks.

I was nervous about going, I didn't want to get there and regret ever leaving. I knew how easy it was to get sucked back into that lifestyle. A lifestyle which was okay if you were rich and famous, not so great for people like me. I spent the whole time visiting friends and eating out. My friend Dean had booked tickets for us to see Rod Stewart play at the Hollywood Bowl. What should have been a great concert turned out to be a real bust. He turned up an hour late and finished it on time, when people expected an encore he came back on stage and said "Now you can all just F*** off". Guess he'd had a bad day. No surprise, I haven't bought tickets to any more of his concerts. I told my friend about the manuscript and he was very encouraging and supportive. Did I regret my decision to leave? Actually no. Yes I had a great time and it was lovely seeing everyone. Home is where the heart is, my home and heart will always be in England.

I'd only been home a few days when I received a call from Dean telling me he'd found a publisher interested in my book. Honestly I never thought about getting it published, it was my way of keeping my stories, my memories, alive. It wasn't even ready to publish. The writing needed polishing grammatically, and the spelling. Now I was feeling a mixture of anxiety and excitement. The only way I can describe the next year of my life is to say it was like a rollercoaster ride. Highs and lows. Because Dean was a hairdresser in Beverly Hills, and we all know what gossips they can be. He told a lady who works for the L.A. Times newspaper, that I was looking for a publisher for my tell-all book.

I had arranged another visit to Los Angeles ands this time I had been told to take my manuscript with me. Dean picked me up from the airport and confessed he'd made an appointment for me to be interviewed for an article that would appear in the L.A. Times. The lady in question was Ann O'Neill, and after the interview I felt like I'd been coerced into a lot of the answers I gave. The next meeting I had was with a lawyer friend of Dean's, again another one of his hair clients. Steve loved what he read and said he already had some interest from a publisher. I came back to England and let them get on with things. Dean sent me a copy of the L.A. Times article, some of the words had been put in my mouth. An email appeared in my box later from Wendy. It read, *call me regarding the book you are writing about the Hiltons." They are very sad, as they really loved you and wondered what they had done to you to have you turn on them like this".*

The email really hit home, I began to wonder if writing this story was really worth causing so much pain to people who in spite of the anxiety they had caused me in the past, in spite of the days I felt like screaming at these people, I did in my own way love them too. Without the Hilton's I would have no story to tell, they gave me a home and a great job. Even after they left Los Angeles they still got me jobs with friends, and Mr H had given me a receptionist position at his real estate office, so how could I let this story go to print, did they really deserve my disloyalty?

I was being suffocated, I felt like I was already in too deep. The publisher had hired someone to ghost write the book. My lawyer was working as a favour to Dean, expecting to be paid once the deal was sealed. I was receiving three-way conversations between Steve and the New York publisher. The prospects of my book being published had become alarmingly real.

The publishers wanted me to embellish any stories I had about Paris, and at the time I didn't understand why all our conversations veered towards questions about her. That was until I heard about her sex tape. I always knew Paris was a little promiscuous, but a sex tape!

Her boyfriend at the time was Rick Solomon and they had made the tape together in a hotel room. It had of course gone viral and catapulted Paris to fame. The tape was entitled *"One Night in Paris"*, I know, very classy. Papa Barron must have been so proud of his granddaughter. Hearing this news I realised that the Hilton's reputation and name was already in the toilet. So me writing a book about this dysfunctional family was just a small drop of poop in what was an enormous ocean of crap.

Right from Day One I wanted the book to be about, my story. The amazing adventure I had been on. "A young woman", well at the time I was. A young woman from a small city in England had arrived in America thinking she would stay for a short time and hopefully would be able to visit some great touristy places. Her life changing so dramatically it all seemed surreal. That's what I wanted the book to be about, not a book aimed as fodder for social media. Not about Paris Bloody Hilton. I'm saying I wanted it to be about me, not to be egotistical. I know it might sound like that. Let me explain. I'm not a journalist, I have no wish to be rich or famous. I don't want to support the tabloid press in an y way, shape or form. I just wanted to tell my story, a story that to me was worth telling. I didn't care if the reader thought its content was made up or embellished in any way. I was truthfully telling my story. If it wouldn't sell because I didn't write enough about Miss Hilton, well quite honestly I didn't give a rat's furry ass. My diary, my story, how dare they try and take that away from me.

This was the roller coaster I was telling you about, and I was beginning to throw up on this ride. Between the publishers pushing me to write crap in my book and the media asking me questions, mainly about Miss Hilton, I was beginning to wish I'd never written my story, or at least not mentioned it to anyone, just kept it to myself. I royally pissed off the publisher, I wasn't going to work with any ghost writer. That coupled with the Hilton's having words in the right ears, put the kybosh on the whole deal. I was relieved in the end, like I said it was never meant to be the type of book that destroyed people's reputations.

I still had calls about the book months after I'd shelved the whole idea of getting it published, I even had a call from Entertainment Tonight. This was a show that aired every evening in Los Angeles and was probably famous throughout the world. They wanted to interview me regarding being nanny to the Hilton girls. My lawyer had told me to do it because it would cause another buzz about my book.

I don't know why I agreed, I had already decided to shelve the whole book deal debacle. They had an office in London and sent a crew over from there to interview me. My little flat in Taverham, Norwich. You couldn't swing a cat round in my little home and it was going to be filled with cameras and TV crew. What a joke. I was a bag of nerves, they asked me some very stupid questions and tried desperately to put words in my mouth. When they left they told me that I would be informed as to when it would be aired. I was just pleased it wouldn't be aired in this country. Turned out it didn't get aired in America either. They told me there had been a technical problem, but I knew the truth. I hadn't given them the answers they needed, this show was Entertainment Tonight and my answers were honest. I didn't attack anyone's character or belittle them. So this didn't make for good TV. At the end of the day who cared? Not me. I took my manuscript and stuck it in the cupboard to gather dust. On rare occasions I would tell the odd story or two, but mainly I just get on with my life.

My visits to Los Angeles became fewer over the years. I went to see my dear friend Mindy in Hawaii a few times and stopped over in L.A. for a few days, mainly to break up the journey. Her home was amazing and her decision to leave Los Angeles and her then cramped house was the best decision she ever made. She was working in a shop and selling the Jams World clothing she had once sold in her own shop. Her life was blessed and I was so happy for her. I did all the touristy things with her. We went on a coach trip up to the Volcano Kīlaueu, the world's most active volcano. Amazing sight.

Just down the road from her was The Hilton Waikoloa Village Resort. This was an amazing place. A beautiful exotic bird welcomed you as you entered the foyer of the hotel. There were man-made beaches, and dolphins swimming in a pool that you could get up close and personal with. They would come up to the side so you could rub their nose. Paying to swim with them was also a possibility, unfortunately I didn't have a swimsuit with me. I did spend a serious amount of money in the amazing shops.

On one of my stop-overs in Los Angeles we decided to go to Las Vegas again. I hadn't been in a while and always loved winning in the MGM Grand Hotel's slots. I had given up on the idea of winning, I had set myself a target on the spend and had reached it, so I went to bed. In the morning I decided to have just one last try, $20 that was all. I came away from there $1500 richer, yes! My third big win on those beautiful machines.

The last time I was in Los Angeles was in 2009, I had been working for a nice company in their office, a very nice well-paid job, but I had burnt myself out, working too many hours. I didn't want to return to Los Angeles on a permanent basis, nor did I want to venture somewhere new. I decided to put all my belongings into storage and go back for just four months. You know when you have the feeling the God's are trying to tell you something. Well just about everything went wrong from Day One.

I stepped down from the coach at the airport and twisted my ankle. I had on these crazy stupid wedged shoes, they were not made for a woman my age. Learned a lesson there the hard way. I bought some flip-flops in the airport, I always thought the word flip-flop cries out, *cheap shoes*. These were by Donna Karan and cost £58.00. What a great start to my trip, excuse the pun. These designer shoes were not going to improve my look. My ankle had swelled up in a grotesque manner and the Quasimodo limp didn't add any finesse to me look. At the boarding-gate it was touch and go as to whether they'd even let me on the plane. They did, and the air crew were amazing all through the flight. They came with ice every hour or so to keep the swelling to a minimum. By the time we reached Los Angeles airport, my ankle was black. I did struggle to put my weight on it. A taxi ride and a flight of stairs later, I was finally at my apartment.

Great start to my holiday, I couldn't leave the apartment for the first three weeks. I wanted to visit friends, one couple especially, neighbours of mine. We had gone everywhere together when I lived there previously. Now Chuck had developed Alzheimer's and Denise had put him in a care home. I wanted to go with her to visit him, as I knew it would probably be the last time I would see him. Turned out I never did get to say goodbye, because he died the same weekend I arrived. Denise had a memorial service for him, and by that time I was able to walk, so I did get to say goodbye, just not in the way I would have liked.

A month already gone and I hadn't done any of the things I had on my list. At least I could get a nice tan so I sat out in the garden sunbathing. A dog was barking on a balcony in a building opposite and I noticed he was jumping up to the rail. Denise came out and we nervously watched this dog jumping potentially to his death. The building was several stories high and this apartment was on the eighth floor. We made a decision to go round and see if there was a concierge at the building. Thinking he could contact the owner and warn him about his dog's possible suicide attempts. Just as we were leaving, the dog stopped and we realised he had gone back in the apartment through the open glass door. What a relief.

I was having a cuppa the next morning on our balcony when I heard the dog barking again. I went in the garden to look and Denise came out, as we both looked up at the building the dog managed to jump up and over the rail. We both screamed and ran round to the building. I went to see the concierge to tell him what had happened. I couldn't go and see the poor dog, I knew he had to be dead. We gave him our name and address in case the owner wanted to know what had happened.

He did come over to speak to us, he was very teary and blaming himself for the poor dog's demise. We didn't confess to him that we had seen his dog jumping up the day before. Because we both felt so guilty, knowing that maybe we could have prevented this horrible accident.

Sunbathing had now been tarnished with the memory of this horrible incident. I found myself constantly looking up at the balcony. I was out in the garden trying to get all these images out of my head when a number of helicopters flew overhead. Helicopters circling over Beverly Hills was not unusual, if there was anyone visiting or there was an award ceremony, let's face it there was always some kind of award ceremony going on. However this was different. They were circling a lot and there was more than one. They didn't let up, so I went inside to turn on the television, if anything exciting was happening, it would always be on the box.

I found myself staring at the TV in shock. Michael Jackson had died. It was June 25th and he had died at his home in Holmby Hills. The world was in shock. Every channel covered this story. Michael Jackson's entire life and death was on display for the media to scrutinize and pick apart. Everyone had an opinion. On August 28th the Los Angeles Coroner concluded that his death was a homicide. His personal physician, Conrad Murray, was convicted of Involuntary Manslaughter in 2011 and served two years of a four-year sentence, receiving early release for good behaviour.

There was a memorial service at the Staples Centre on July 7th, I didn't go to that. But I did walk into Beverly Hills because I knew there was something happening at the Wilshire Beverly Hotel, I did see a lot of people in black coming out of the back entrance of the hotel, there were many photographers there.

Denise and I had spoken about me making good memories. We made a list of many touristy things that I could do. I hadn't been to the Hollywood Wax Works, or the Kodak Centre. We went to look at the many flowers placed on the handprints of Michael Jackson, on the Hollywood Walk of Fame. It was crowded, so much so they had placed railings round the prints so people walked round in single file, preventing congestion. Another day we went over to Michael's Holmby Hills home, morbid fascination I guess. The gates leading into the property displayed a cornucopia of flowers.

Another day we went stalking. Yes that's what I said, stalking. We acted like a couple of giddy schoolgirls. I had the address of many movie stars and we thought we'd see what their homes looked like. David Beckham had a home there at the time, because he was playing for L.A. Galaxy. We did get really near to his home. And then there was Tom Cruise's home. The crème de la crème was the home of Johnny Depp. Be still my beating heart. We parked outside his home, it was surrounded by high gates and hedges. We knew he was probably in town as he'd been promoting his new movie, *Public Enemies.* So we thought we'd sit for a while, in case he appeared. The home was on a slope and we couldn't see if anyone was coming down the hill, till they were on top of us. Suddenly a golf cart appeared and a man asked us what we were doing. I joked that we were stalking Johnny Depp. This man was not amused, he was Mr Depp's security and asked us to move on.

My holiday was coming to an end. I'd had a lot of fun with Denise, she had helped me gain some really great memories to take home. So in spite of the bad start, with the ankle and the horrendous dog incident, I'd had a brilliant time.

I only had a few days left and feeling I'd almost completed my wish list, I decided that the last few days should be spent shopping. Denise came over to see me and said that Johnny Depp's new movie was premiering in Westwood at the Mann Theatre. She knew that seeing him would be the icing on my cake. The premiere would take place early evening and Denise had read that Johnny Depp and all the other actors in the movie would be on the red carpet. Westwood had some great shops and lots of places to eat, so I knew I could get a lift there quite early from Dean, and hang out there until the premiere. That's what I did, got a lift in late morning and went straight to the Mann's Theatre to see how many people were already waiting there.

It was already filling up, even with six hours to go. I wanted to be in a position to see Mr Depp but I couldn't imagine getting a spot and not wanting to give it up to go to the toilet, or eat anything.

Most of these people were with friends, so their friends could hold their spot for them. I was on my own, so had no such luxury. I went and had some lunch, went to the loo and purchased some bottled water. Things had really filled up now and I nearly gave up the whole idea. I wandered round to try and see if there was anywhere that I could get in a good position, where my view wasn't blocked. Being only five foot tall was definitely a disadvantage.

At the back of the Mann's Theatre was a queue of people. There was a beginning and an end., but no sign telling anyone what it was for. I guessed the people in it knew why they were lined up, at least you'd hope so. They were all quite young and part of me thought they might be auditioning for something. Curiosity got the better of me, so I asked this young girl who was standing at the end, what the line was for. "This is the line for the red carpet stands", she said. Of course I knew what they were. Not. After seeing the dumb blank look on my face, she explained that the stands that were either side of the red carpet had to be filled by fans. This was the line of fans that hoped to fill those seats. Hey, I had nothing to lose so I joined the line. Now this girl was no novice, she joined many a line and had come from Las Vegas to join this one. She went on to tell me that most people didn't know that anyone could get onto the stands, it was a secret these veteran fans kept to themselves. I was so grateful she'd let me in on it.

She told me that the real nerve-wracking part came later. The organisers would pick the first eighty or so from the line and the rest would be left out. She had sent her husband down to the front to count how many people were in the queue before us. When he came back he said it was really tight, but he thought we would just be alright. I kept the drinking of water down to a minimum, I was in this great position now and didn't want to lose it. The time came for them to start letting us in to fill the seats. Her husband was right, it was tight but we managed tio get in with just a handful of people behind us having the same luck.

We couldn't sit just anywhere, we had to move along filling each bench until that block was full, then they filled the next and so on. I was lucky to be on the second row and I had an amazing view of the red carpet. Definitely no going to the toilet now. It seemed like forever for them to arrive and *Entertainment Tonight* and many other camera and TV film crews were there. So we had to go through photographs and interviews with all the other actors before we got to see Mr Depp himself. Looking gorgeous as ever, I took some photos and when he waved at us all on the bench, I knew he was waving at me. Well in my dreams anyway. It was all over too quickly. I left the stand elated. It was getting chilly and I had a sleeveless dress on, so I was rushing to a phone box so I could call Denise to come and pick me up. I couldn't wait to tell her the position I'd been in, the red carpet no less. As I was crossing the road a black car was driving slowly by. It had blacked-out windows and I found myself starting at them. Then the window began to slide down and a smiling face was looking at me, that face belonged to Mr Depp. That was my last surreal moment in La La Land. I was beside myself with delight and also a little confused as to why he hadn't gone into the cinema to see his movie. I later learned that he never does.

Johnny Depp on the red carpet, dancing with the news presenter.

Johnny, so near, almost within touching distance.

Johnny, walking towards where I was sitting in the stands.

So to sum things up. At the start of this holiday things had really gone badly for me. Then it turned out to be pretty amazing. At last I got my happy ending.

That's the end of my story about living in La La Land. Warts and all.

Postscript

I thought I might end this book with an update, especially as this is now March 2023. Yes it had been over thirty years since I stepped out of that plane at LAX. The movie *Pretty Woman* still playing in my mind. Those famous words announced at the end. "Welcome to Hollywood, what's your dream?". A lifetime ago and seems like yesterday.

As I'm sure you know, Paris has made a name for herself after the whole sex tape incident. It was never enough for her to just be known as one of the heirs to the Hilton Fortune. This girl had to stand out and she certainly achieved that. I never saw the video, someone at work was playing it when I arrived at work, one morning. Purely to play a joke on me. I was never going to watch a girl I had known from the age of nine having sex.

Then she appeared on my TV screen in a little drama called *Simple Life*. Drama, comedy, reality show, no one could be sure which genre this belonged in. I wasn't even certain whether the word simple, referred to the actors, or the lifestyle, or both. Anyway it starred Paris and her best friend, Nicole Richie. I had to watch it, even though it was cringeingly bad acting and boring rubbish. I was lured in by the knowledge that I personally knew these girls. Now here they were on my TV in my home in England. So I got hooked on the rubbish and it ran for five series until 2007. Nicole Richie went on to marry Joel Madden and have two children.

Paris had some bad relationships that didn't last. Despite zero percent common sense, she did amaze me by becoming quite an established and successful business woman. She has amassed quite a nice fortune. She can't act or sing. But has earned money from both. She now DJ's all over the world and apparently designs stuff. Now forty-two years old, she has a husband, Carter Reum, and a child they named Phoenix Barron Hilton Reum. She's published three books, the latest being her memoirs. Way to go, Paris.

Nicky achieved this and much more, earlier on. The one Hilton I loved, and I am so pleased that she did get her dream. She made it first as a great designer. Then she had a small hiccup marrying in Las

Vegas briefly, and another to get said marriage annulled. Then along came her prince, James Rothschild. This guy is heir to the Rothschild fortune and we are not talking millions, this family make the Hilton's look like paupers because we are talking trillions. They now have three children, Lily Grace Victoria born July 2016, Teddy Marilyn born December 20th 2018 and Caspian Barron born July 2022. They seem very happy and I know Nicky is still an amazing designer. Paris may have been a little jealous of her sister for a while there.

Still I'm guessing not so jealous of her brothers though. Barron, although now seems to be settled down, had a very wild youth. He had a D.U.I. in 2008 at just eighteen years old. Then another incident where he said he was attacked by friends of Lindsay Lohan at a mansion.

Now this bad boy made good is married to socialite, Tessa Grafin von Walderdorff, I know what a flippin' mouthful. Let's hope he just calls her Tess or Waldo.

The fourth Hilton Conrad. I never really knew him, he was the one Mum and Dad welcomed into the world with a birthing party, and Chasen's catered the event, remember. I wonder if his bizarre entry into this world scarred him for life. Because this brother finishes up in jail. He had a drug-fuelled meltdown on a flight. The flight was from London to Los Angeles and a witness gave details of the meltdown in court. He smoked weed in the toilets and then threatened the flight staff. "I will fucking own anyone on this flight, they are all peasants". He also said he could get them all fired in five minutes and that his father would pay this out, he had done it before, he paid out $300,000 last time. These were just some of his rantings. He tried to punch fellow passengers and threatened to kill several of the flight attendants. He left the plane in handcuffs. Looks like Daddy had another fine to pay.

Still keeping with this family. I turned my TV on one afternoon and two faces jumped off the screen, flooding me with memories. Kyle and Kim Richards, the two sisters of Kathy Hilton. Starring in a reality show called, *Real Housewives of Beverly Hills.* There they were playing out all their dramas. Firstly let me just say I would love to meet the numpty who titled this show. Please! REAL nothing real about any of these women. HOUSEWIVES. Definition in my dictionary: A woman whose main occupation is looking after her family and the home. A more realistic title would be, Rich socialites who bitch a lot in Beverly Hills. Not quite as catchy though I guess. Truth is these women do not take care of their children or homes, they have nannies and maids to do that. Their days consist of shopping in designer boutiques, meeting friends for coffee or lunch or spending the day at a spa. Who can blame them, they are rich and can afford to do these things. But don't call them Real Housewives, it's an insult to Real Housewives. Rant over.

I still watch the show, if only to see how Kyle, Kim and Kathy "who has now succumbed to the lure of the show" are getting on. It's also nice to see the children all grown up.

Sadly a few of the people mentioned in my story have passed away. Dudley Moore, the great man has joined Peter Cook, his partner in comedy for many years. Walter Matthau and Jack Lemmon, another comedy duo, together again. Ed McMahon died June 23rd 2009 and sadly Victoria joined him on 15th July 2016.

The saddest death for me was the loss of an angel from this earth. My dear friend Connie Pentek, the lady that helped keep me sane through all the Hilton dramas, that made me laugh, rather than cry. The lady that told me I should write a book.